The Dynamics of Business Communication

The Dynamics of Business Communication

How to Communicate Efficiently and Effectively

John Kennedy

www.studymates.co.uk

© 2009 Studymates Limited for cover and page design

ISBN: 978-1-84285-139-5

Website@ www.studymates.co.uk

Note: The contents of this book are offered for the purposes of general guidance only and no liability can be accepted for any loss or expense incurred as a result of relying in particular circumstances on statements made in this book. Readers are advised to take professional advice where necessary before entering into personal arrangements.

Typeset by Vikatan Publishing Solutions, Chennai, India
Printed and bound in Europe

Contents

Introduction

The dynamics of business communication.

From early theorists such as Aristotle to modern social scientists, studies of communication can be seen to have undergone a number of significant changes—from a focus on the strategies and skills of communication (Aristotle), to an emphasis on how messages are transmitted (Shannon and Weaver); and finally, to attempts at understanding the nature of meaning and impact of communication on the receiver (Harold Lasswell). For example, whereas natural scientists like Claude Shannon held that communication was the transmission and reception of information, social scientists viewed communication as the generation and understanding of meaning. One way of accommodating both views is to see communication as the management of messages for the purpose of creating meaning and understanding.

Many of the concepts developed by early researchers and theorists of communication can be seen to underpin many of the practices of business organisations today. Whether in an internal organisational sense, where radical change is fundamental to success (or even survival), or in an external sense to improve market share, organisations and leaders must be credible. In addition to business competence, the basis of this credibility for staff and the general public is very often the same qualities identified by Aristotle: personal character, logical analysis and appropriate emotional appeal—key aspects of persuasion.

As well as being crucial for leadership, principles like those established by Aristotle and modern theorists can be seen to be vital for persuasion in a different context. Marketing, advertising and public relations professionals need to be able to understand how to maximise the impact of their message: how is the message best constructed, what is the best way to transmit it, what impact will it have? These questions and more can be answered by examining the communication principles established through many years of research.

The increasing complexity of modern business organisations, exemplified by the rise of the computer and associated developments such as email, video conferencing, the internet and e-commerce, has meant that the technological aspects of business communication have assumed a prominence that threatens the human element. Project-based work, the importance of teamwork, and the rise of the service sector with its demand for sound interpersonal skills should remind organisations that the human aspects of communication are to be ignored at the peril of the business. All of these issues are compounded by intensive competition. In most sectors, business organisations stand or fall by their communication competence.

Understanding the dynamics of business communication entails an examination of areas not directly associated with it. Accordingly, this book will consider and develop areas such as motivation, trust and self-development. Why? Because these areas are crucially linked to issues such as self-confidence; this in turn has a significant impact on the way we communicate, and the way *our communication is perceived by others*.

Importantly, the key skills associated with communication in general are transferable to the personal as well as the work setting. Therefore, by mastering the communication skills necessary for working life, individuals maximise their communication impact in their personal lives.

This book is designed to help meet the ever-increasing need for business and personal communication competence by enabling you to:

- Understand current communication themes better, by explaining the development of theory
- Realise the importance and essence of communication in organisations
- Develop important personal and communication skills
- Recognise the importance of trust, and how it can be developed and maintained
- Appreciate the importance of factors such as customer care
- Examine key aspects of particular 'messages', and how these can be improved
- Focus on employees and how their contribution to the business can be maximised
- Grasp the significance of marketing communications
- Understand key elements of crisis management such as the crisis communication plan
- Meet the communication challenges of cyberspace

John Kennedy MBA
John.kennedy@studymates.co.uk

1 Communication theory

One-minute overview

As indicated in the introduction, communication theory can be seen to be the foundation upon which modern concepts of communication are based. Early theorists such as Aristotle highlighted the important trio of person, message and audience. In the technical age, transmission theorists emphasised the importance of how the message was transmitted; and social scientists focused on the crucial elements of meaning and impact on those who receive the message. To understand how communication theory developed, is to understand the necessary factors for effective business communication

This chapter will enable you to:

- Understand that communication is a skills-based activity
- Realise the importance of considering message elements such as content, method, meaning and impact
- Be aware that communication can be broken down into key elements such as person, message and audience
- Appreciate that rhetorical devices can be used in modern business practice
- Recognise the significance of attitudes, values and beliefs with regard to communication
- Value the importance of interpersonal skills, and the human need for affection and inclusion

Communication is the principal mechanism through which human relations exist, develop and perpetuate. Purposeful and meaningful communication in different forms (e.g. speech and writing) is the key factor that separates human beings from all other species. Other species such as animals communicate purposely and effectively (e.g. displaying affection, warning of danger etc.), but only mankind has such an elaborate repertoire of communicating behaviour at its disposal. Communication is such an ever-present part of our daily lives that even deciding not to communicate is in itself a form of communication.

Consciously or unconsciously, business organisations rely on years of research in order to target key internal and external audiences. The growth in sophisticated communication technology and expertise has been matched by a growing sophistication of the audiences themselves. Whether internal or external, audiences have been exposed to many years of communication in various forms. Subjected daily to radio, television and print media, audiences have come to expect high standards on the part of the business communicator.

Modern communication technology, whilst having considerable benefits such as maximising impact and saving time, can also be seen to have significant drawbacks.

For example, emails have revolutionised personal and business communication in the same manner as the telegraph did in the 19th C. At the same time, however, they can be seriously misused, occupy large amounts of employee time, can contain irrelevant information and can cause situations that breach the laws of confidentiality and the Data Protection Act.

In addition to these important issues, modern technology like computers has undermined communication methods that have a greater degree of personal impact (such as meetings and the telephone).

As communication technology has advanced, so too has the theory; indeed, there are almost as many communication theories as there are methods. However, in order to more fully understand the demands, processes and impact of the modern business organisation in communication terms, it is necessary to 'go back to the future'; to briefly chart the evolution of communication theory from early figures such as Aristotle, to more recent commentators of the twentieth century.

1.1 Aristotle and rhetoric

Ancient philosophers such as Aristotle, Plato and Cicero viewed communication as critical for anyone engaged in public life, and invested a great deal of time and effort in order to develop a better understanding of the concepts and skills involved. In particular, Aristotle can be seen to have established the fundamental principles of persuasion that are used by many business communicators today.

Aristotle and others focused on the skills of what was known in the ancient world as rhetoric; the ability to make powerful speeches in public. In the ancient world (particularly Greece), the ability to have an impact on large groups through the ability to speak effectively (rhetoric), was considered a divine gift. For Aristotle, the key to effective rhetoric was the ability to identify, in a particular case, the best means of persuasion.

As figure 1 illustrates, Aristotle held that there were three main aspects to successful rhetoric:

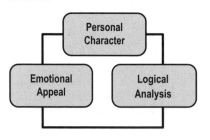

Ethos – the personal character or appeal of the speaker

Logos – the logic and interest of the argument

Pathos – the appeal to people's emotions

No matter how sophisticated modern communication models have become, many can be seen to include these three components.

Figure 1: Aristotle's model of rhetoric.

Thus, Aristotle's model of rhetoric is a significant contribution to our understanding of the development of the communication process, and a key underlying feature of contemporary business communication. As figure 1 confirms, Aristotle believed that rhetoric is a skills-based activity that requires proficiency across a number of key areas:

Innovation and organisation – the ability to generate and organise ideas
Memory – the ability to recall facts effectively
Communication style – the use of appropriate language
Delivery – maximising the above through the use of voice, gestures and non-verbal behaviour

Aristotle analysed not only the actual skills of rhetoric, but other key aspects like the character of the individual (their 'believability factor'), the logic of the argument or points made, and the extent to which statements appealed to the emotions of the listeners. Aristotle's work, where rhetoric is concerned, is more than a study of 'a person of good character speaking well'. His focus on rhetoric provided the first systematic study of the art of persuasion, and also emphasised that communication is purposive. For instance, it is based on the notion of affecting others, and that the effects of communication can be measured. In addition, Aristotle's seminal thoughts on the persuasive aspects of communication confirm that communication can go beyond mere information-giving; they consider not only what is or was, but also what might be. This is especially so, when individuals seek to improve the human experience:

Some men see things as they are, and say why?
I dream things that never were and say why not?

Robert F Kennedy
(previously stated by George Bernard Shaw)

Aristotle also identified aspects of communication style that aided the impact of the speaker: purity or correctness of language; clarity; what he termed 'ornaments' (figures of speech); question types; and rhetorical devices. Figure 2 represents some of the devices that Aristotle and other early communication theorists held to be crucial for effective persuasion. Some of the great orators through the years have used these devices.

Abraham Lincoln, perhaps one of the greatest orators of all time, had a particularly powerful impact on audiences because he used rhetorical devices along with simple language. The following words from the Gettysburg Address are an example of the use of *asyndeton*: *"But in a larger sense, we cannot dedicate, we cannot consecrate, we cannot hallow this ground."*

Similarly, President John F Kennedy used the same technique with equally dramatic results, *"We shall pay any price, bear any burden, meet any hardships, support any friend, oppose any foe to assure the survival and the success of liberty".* The rhetorical device of *anaphora* lies

> **Allegory** – a symbolic narrative
> **Anaphora** – repetition of a word at the beginning of consecutive sentences
> **Asyndeton** – omitting conjunctions between words and phrases
> **Hyperbole** – exaggeration for effect
> **Metaphor** – a word/phrase that implies a likeness between different things
> **Onomatopoeia** – sounds that suggest meaning
> **Syllogism** – a logical argument in three parts (two premises and a conclusion)

Figure 2: Aristotle's rhetorical devices.

at the heart of one of the most significant speeches with regard to human aspiration; the 'I have a dream speech' by Martin Luther King (August 28th, 1963):

I have a dream that one day this nation will rise up
and live out the true meaning of its creed—'we hold
these truths to be self-evident that all men are created equal'

I have a dream that one day on the red hills of Georgia, the
sons of slaves and the sons of slave-owners, will be able to
sit down together at the table of brotherhood

I have a dream that one day, even the state of Mississippi,
sweltering with the heat of injustice, sweltering with the heat
of oppression, will be transformed into an oasis of freedom
and justice

I have a dream today…

Many of the rhetorical devices outlined above can be seen to be the basis of many advertising and public relations campaigns. For example,

'Do you want the best insurance'?
'Do you want the best service'?
'Do you want the lowest premium'?
(use of anaphora);

'probably the best beer in the world'
(use of hyperbole)

'The Meteor has the highest number of safety devices'
'The Meteor has the best safety record of any car'
'The Meteor is the safest car on the roads today'
(use of syllogism)

Another aspect of rhetoric that Aristotle held to be crucial was *eristics;* the ability to argue a case from one position, and then from the opposite one. He believed that eristics was a necessary skill for effective leadership. One of Aristotle's most famous pupils was Alexander the Great, and amongst many other leadership skills, Aristotle taught Alexander the art of eristics. Aristotle's tutelage of Alexander where rhetoric is concerned complemented Alexander's natural ability to communicate, and made him one of the outstanding orators and leaders of his generation.

Modern organisations are particularly concerned with influencing *knowledge, attitudes* and *behaviour*, and Aristotle's thoughts on rhetoric and communication, in general, can be seen to be of crucial importance in this respect. In addition to the above modern aspects of communication, his importance is also based on the following:

1. He was one of the first theorists to identify the key components of *speaker, message* and *audience*
2. He placed particular emphasis on the importance of communication style and the use of evidence
3. The three dimensions of Aristotle's model (ethos, logos and pathos) can be seen to form the basis of a wider communications framework. In its broadest definition, *ethos* includes all the elements of the speaker or writer that influence the communication process. *Logos* can be seen to refer to all the aspects of the message or written text. Finally, in this respect, *pathos* can be held to relate to all the dimensions of the audience. No matter how sophisticated modern communication models have become then, most can be seen to include these three key elements

Thus, Aristotle's model of rhetoric and the accompanying principles are a significant contribution to our understanding of the communication process and its subsequent development. His formative work is a key underlying feature of many aspects of business communication today.

1.2 The development of communication theory

In a more modern sense, the development of communication theory occurred principally in the United States, and there were three main strands to this. Firstly, in the early 1900s, educationalists who stressed the importance of oral communication tended to be frowned upon by other academics who viewed literature as the most important aspect of communication. In response to this, and in order to be seen as more 'scientific', academics associated with the spoken word founded the Speech Association of America. To support the Association, a new journal, The Quarterly Journal of Public Speaking, was also founded.

By the mid-twenties, the new scholarly field of rhetorical criticism had been developed. This was based on the belief that, unlike literature, oral communication in a public setting was concerned with *effect*. A cornerstone of the new field was the belief that communication to a specific audience could be analysed in terms of the orator's method. In many respects, the new academic field was 'Aristotle re-visited'; it viewed oral communication in the form of rhetorical discourse as an art, rather than a science. In this form, the critical study of speech was to dominate communication theory for many years.

The second strand of the development of communication theory was given impetus by World War Two. Prior to this period, few scholars would have referred to their scholarly activity as communication research. Much of the research in the field was conducted under the auspices of social science departments such as sociology, psychology and political science. However, in addition to weapons and munitions, the modern practice of war also required the maximisation of influence, support and the control of information. President F D Roosevelt had already demonstrated the power of mass communication in his radio-delivered 'fireside chats'. His famous quote, "We have nothing to fear but fear itself", became a rallying cry for lifting America out of the depths of economic depression.

Four key figures emerged during this second strand of communication research: Harold Laswell (political scientist), Kurt Lewin (social psychologist), Paul Lazarfield (sociologist) and Carl Hoveland (experimental psychologist). These scholars made the following significant contributions to communication research:

Harold Lasswell Lasswell analysed the content of Nazi propaganda to determine why it had such a powerful effect on those who experienced it. Mainly as a result of this work, he determined that the communication process consisted of five key elements: *who*, says *what*, through *which channel*, to *whom*, with what *effect*.

Kurt Lewin Having escaped Hitler's holocaust, Lewin had a strong dislike of authoritarian leaders. Consequently, he focused on prejudice and the way in which groups influence the decisions of individual members (later referred to as 'group think').

Paul Lazarfield Lazarfield's pioneering Radio Research Project investigated the emotional impact of broadcasting. His work on marketing issues presented by clients was one of the first links between communication research and business practice.

Carl Hoveland Whilst Hoveland's work investigating the effects of the *Why We Fight* films on soldier morale was important in itself, it reflected his pre-occupation with the study of the pervasive effects of source credibility and the sequencing of arguments and evidence within a message (back to Aristotle again).

*Another key figure associated with this movement, Wilbur Schramm, will be referred to later

The Shannon and Weaver model

In experiments at the Bell Telephone Company aimed at optimising telephone signals, Claude Shannon unknowingly initiated the third strand of communication research. In 1949, working with another electrical engineer (Warren Weaver), Shannon was concerned with discovering how much information (coded within a signal system) could be transmitted through a channel of communication. A mathematician by training, Shannon was trying to formulate a theory that would help engineers to find the most efficient way of transmitting electrical signals from one source to another. In other words, getting maximum telephone line capacity with minimum distortion.

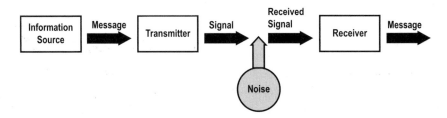

Figure 3: The Shannon & Weaver model of communication.

As Figure 3 shows, the Shannon-Weaver model of communication focuses purely on the transmission and reception of information. As such, models like these are known as 'transmission models'. Although such models later had a feedback loop added, the original model, as represented above, had a number of limitations:

- It focuses only on the technical aspects of communication
- It views communication as a one-way linear process
- It omits the important elements of message content, meaning and feedback
- Apart from the 'noise' element, it conveys the image of a communication process that is simple and without problems

The Shannon-Weaver model was based on the premise of limiting information loss by minimising electrical noise. Indeed, it might be more accurate to describe the model as one of information theory rather than communication. Despite the above limitations, Shannon and Weaver's model was of great significance. Firstly, the original meaning of electrical noise was extended to include any distortion that detracts from the message. Secondly, it helped to highlight the view that communication is a process that includes important elements like *source, encoding*, the *message* itself, the *channel* used, *decoding* the message and *receiving*. Thirdly, it served to later emphasise the criticality of feedback. Fourthly, the work of Shannon and Weaver led to research into how communication physically manifests itself (e.g. powerful images). One important example of such research was the work of George Gerbner. Working in 1956, Gerbner extended Shannon and Weaver's ideas to include the elements of perception, context of the message and reactions to Situations.

Harold Laswell's 1948 model

Laswell, whose five key elements of *who, says what*, through *which channel*, to *whom*, with what *effect* were mentioned earlier, was one of the first of the modern communication theorists to focus on what impact the particular communication had on the receiver. Because of his interest in mass communication and propaganda, Laswell's work was largely associated with control analysis. In an age of intensive mass

Figure 4: Laswell's 1948 model of communication.

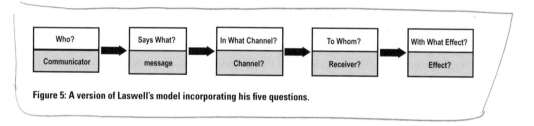

Figure 5: A version of Laswell's model incorporating his five questions.

communication, Laswell's research causes us to ask searching questions about the almost constant barrage of media messages that impact our daily lives.

Laswell's five key questions were later extended to include:

- Under what circumstances?
- For what purpose?
- Who decides what the message is?
- What are their aims?
- Who owns the medium? (e.g. radio, television, newspaper)
- What are their political views/allegiances?

Osgood and Schramm

Working with Charles Osgood, Wilbur Schramm was one of the first communication researchers to improve upon the mathematical model of Shannon and Weaver. Schramm made three important innovations. Firstly, he asserted that the encoding and decoding processes occurred simultaneously by both sender and receiver. Secondly, he allowed for a two-way interchange of messages. Thirdly, he tackled the issue of meaning by providing the process of interpretation. For Schramm, factors such as relations were

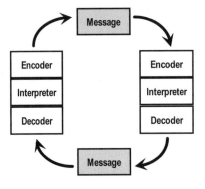

Figure 6: Osgood and Schramm's model (1954).

crucial. If the encoder's and decoder's field of experience overlap (shared meaning), then effective communication can occur.

However, if there is only a small overlap, then communication is difficult, if not impossible. Osgood and Schramm's model is based on the belief that each individual in the communication process possesses the ability to both send and receive (encode and decode). As indicated above, each person's experiences critically influences the way in which symbols (e.g. verbal and non-verbal) are interpreted. To sum up this important aspect of Osgood and Schramm's work, the communication only has meaning if the individual's prior experiences provide a basis for understanding the communication.

Mini Glossary
Channel: The medium of communication through which information is transmitted
Communication effects: the impact on the receiver in intellectual, emotional or behavioural terms
Decoding: interpreting the symbols or signs used by the sender of a message
Encoding: how information is transmitted, and how the signal or message may contain values, attitudes or beliefs
Noise: anything that interferes with effective communication

An important strength of Schramm's work is the notion of how values, beliefs and attitudes affect the communication process. However, although Osgood and Schramm's model allows for the vital factor of feedback between the two parties, it does not embrace the view that communication can occur at multiple levels.

Berlo's S-M-C-R model

Developed in 1960, David Berlo's model has been held by some as the simplest, yet most influential, model for many years. From Berlo's perspective, our skill as a communicator is crucial to the whole process. Like Schramm, Berlo held that our ability to encode messages depends not only on finding the

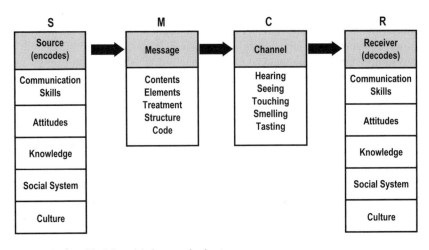

Figure 7: An adaption of Berlo's model of communication.

right words (from our point of view), but of finding words that have a common meaning for the receiver as well.

Similarly, deficiencies in our conceptual powers limit the range of ideas to be communicated in the first place. Berlo uses the word *treatment* to refer to the process whereby the source (or sender) makes decisions about selecting and arranging the code and content of the message.

In addition to its simplicity, Berlo's model was viewed as significant because:

- The idea of 'source' was flexible enough to include media such as oral, written and electronic
- It emphasised the transmission of ideas by making the 'message' the central element
- It highlighted the fact that the codes people use tend to reflect the way they see the world
- It emphasised the importance of *how* the message is encoded for successful communication
- The human senses (e.g. seeing, hearing, touching) were added as a channel factor

Interestingly, Berlo took the view that verbal communication skills were comprised of the following:

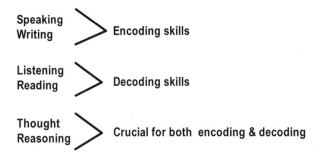

People's attitudes are formed in a variety of ways: their self-image; their view of the message; their opinion of the receiver. In Berlo's model, the receiver is influenced by the same factors; therefore, even the simplest of messages can be a very complex affair, where encoding, decoding, encoding, etc. occurs and recurs as the communication continues. Attitudes can also be seen in terms of three key elements: the *affective* (feelings), the *cognitive* (beliefs) and the *behavioural* (actions).

In addition to the positive factors already outlined, Berlo's views of the encoding and decoding process was a significant improvement on the simple technical-transmission model of Shannon and Weaver. Berlo highlighted the human aspects of communication, and problems of translating thoughts and concepts into meaningful words and symbols that others could understand.

Despite the many positive dimensions of Berlo's work, a number of criticisms can be made. Firstly, his model does tend to give the impression that human communication is machine-like. Secondly, it neglects the fact that even if the right codes are

Mini Glossary
An attitude: being predisposed in a negative or positive way to a message and/or its transmitter
A belief: a position or standard that a person holds to be valid or truthful
A value: a deeply held core belief

used, people can still misunderstand each other. Notwithstanding, and taking all the evidence into consideration, Berlo's S-M-C-R model was a significant development in our understanding of human communication.

1.3 The rise of interpersonal skills

In one respect, of course, the development of interpersonal skills is simply an extension of communication theory. However, the sheer importance of this aspect of communications merits a separate focus. Given the many texts and academic papers that appeared in the late 1950s and 60s, it is understandable that some communication theorists hold that it was the 1960s that gave birth to the interpersonal skills movement. However, the seeds of the interpersonal skills movement were sown much earlier.

There were four main reasons for the increasing interest in interpersonal skills in the 20th century: academic research, a growing recognition of the importance of the human factor in the workplace, the increasing number of 'popular psychology' books on issues associated with interpersonal skills and social change.

Academic research

In the early part of the 20th century, Charles Horton Cooley was interested by how individuals developed their view of themselves (their *self concept*). For Cooley and others, a large part of a person's self concept is formed through their interaction with others; particularly the way in which others react to them in terms of behaviour. For example, individuals who receive positive messages will tend to have a higher self-concept.

> **Mini Glossary**
>
> **Interpersonal skills:** the ability to read and effectively manage the emotions, motivations and behaviours of others duing social interaction
>
> **Higher self concept:** people who experience positive responses and behaviour from others will tend to feel better about themselves

Again, in the early part of the 20th century, sociologist George Herbert Mead was developing his theories of human action and meaning. Mead's key tenets were taken up and further developed by his disciple Herbert Blumer. A key aspect of Blumer's resulting 'symbolic interactionism' theory was the view that human beings are constantly seeking to attach meaning to their social worlds; crucial elements here are *language, meaning* and *thought*.

The 1950s saw an increasing number of figures such as Harry Stack Sullivan develop new theories of communication that related to interpersonal skills. For Sullivan, his field of psychiatry was, in essence, the study of interpersonal relationships. In contrast to theorists such as Freud (who maintained that people are driven by inner instincts and urges), Sullivan held that personality can only be known and understood through the medium of interpersonal interactions.

In the 1960s, the work of William Schutz had a significant impact on the way interpersonal skills research was viewed. Schutz was a leading light in the encounter group movement that advocated the open and honest sharing of feelings—whatever the effect on others. Whilst traditional researchers and others frowned upon the encounter group movement, Schutz himself gained recognition for his theory of

Fundamental Interpersonal Relations Orientation (FIRO). In connection with the FIRO theory, Schutz asserted that all humans possess three key needs to a greater or lesser degree: the need for *inclusion, control* and *affection.*

For Schutz, the need for inclusion was an individual's inner drive to establish and maintain a satisfactory relationship with others. In modern language, it had to do with being either 'in' (one of the 'in-crowd'),

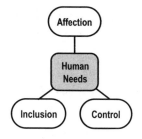

Figure 8: Schutz's human relation needs.

or 'out' (excluded). Schutz maintained that the need for control in the interpersonal context was related to the person's need to form a satisfactory relationship regarding power and control. Whereas the need for inclusion was related to being in or out, Schutz held that the need for love and affection was linked to being close or far in interpersonal terms.

Another important aspect of Schutz's FIRO theory was that, once an individual experienced another in an interpersonal sense, the more easier it was to predict their future behaviour.

The workplace

The recognition of the importance of the human dimension in the workplace was due, firstly, to the emergence of the human relations academic field of study, and secondly, the changing nature of work itself. The human relations school of thought was, in part, a response to the 'scientific management' approach to work, whereby work was broken down into a number of isolated tasks completed by different individuals. Followers of the human relations movement believed that scientific management, developed at the turn of the 20th century, dehumanised workers and treated them like a cog in a machine. A significant milestone in the human relations field was the Hawthorne Experiment. Conducted in the 1920s, by Harvard researchers at the Hawthorne Plant of the Western Electric Company, the series of experiments revealed that when employees feel recognised and important, greater work motivation can result.

In addition to advances in communication theory, the nature of work was changing in a number of respects: it was becoming more sophisticated (e.g. projects and team-working); the rise in the service sector meant a growing need for customer-facing staff with good interpersonal skills; the growing sophistication created a demand for managers with knowledge of managing interpersonal relationships (particularly the ability to motivate others).

Where managers are concerned, the research of Henry Mintzberg was highly significant. Mintzberg believed that a manager's job consisted of three primary roles: The *informational role*, where managers seek and disseminate information necessary for the efficient functioning of the organisation; the *decisional role*, where the information gained is used for purposes such as solving problems and allocating scarce resources; the third role is the crucial one of *interpersonal* relations. A manager's job entails constant personal links between parties like staff, superiors, customers and suppliers. Not only does communication in a general sense underpin all of these roles, but researchers Fred Luthans and Janet Larsen found that, on a typical day, 75% of a manager's communication occurred in face-to-face-situations.

Popular psychology books

There have been a number of popular psychology books that have had quite an impact on the development of the interpersonal skills movement. Whilst Erving Goffman's 1959 book, *The Presentation of Self in Everyday Life* was not as popular outside the academic sphere as some others, it presented the interesting format of the theatrical (dramaturgical) performance as a means of understanding human behaviour.

Goffman took the view that all our actions, and the interpretation and meaning we attach to them, are fundamentally social in nature. Thus, all our actions are social 'performances' with the aim of not only achieving what the action is supposed to achieve, but also of giving off certain impressions to others (what is now called in interpersonal skills terms, *impression management*).

Accordingly, an important focus of Goffman's work was his investigation into how people present themselves in everyday life, and how others perceived them. From Goffman's perspective, the most meaningful individual behaviour occurs in the chance encounters of everyday life; events such as greeting people and casual conversations. Each social encounter (performance) has a structure of its own, and can be examined by the use of 'frames' (reference points).

Published in 1964, Dr Eric Berne's book *Games People Play* is one of the most popular psychology books ever published; worldwide, over five million copies have been sold. The book describes life as a series of games or interactions between two or more people. The interactions can take the form of words, and aspects of non-verbal behaviour such as facial expressions. The ultimate aim of the main player is to achieve some sort of goal (often an emotional one). However, despite the name 'games', the behaviour occurring during the activities can be damaging.

A key concept of Berne's that underpinned his work was Transactional Analysis (TA). From Berne's perspective, TA was both a theory and a process of psychotherapy aimed at personal growth and change. Berne believed that a person experiences and projects his or her personality through a mixture of thoughts, feelings and behaviours. Consequently, some of the key principles associated with TA are as follows:

> **Parent** – This is a state in which people think, feel and behave in response to an unconscious repeat of how their parents or other parental figures acted. People act in this way because they have 'learned' that this is a viable way of relating to others in the circumstances
>
> **Adult** – In this state, people think, feel and behave in response to what is going on in the present. When a person is in the adult state, they are orientated towards an objective review of reality
>
> **Child** – Here, the person reverts to thinking, feeling and behaving similarly to how they thought, felt and behaved in childhood. When experiencing certain situations or behaviour from others, they may engage in 'childish' behaviour
>
> **Strokes** – These are the recognition, attention or responsiveness that one person gives to another. They can be negative or positive. A key premise here is that people crave recognition, and that lacking positive strokes, will engage in negative behaviour in order to achieve recognition
>
> **Transactions** – These are the flows of information that occur at the actual and psychological levels.

In addition to making an important contribution to psychotheraphy and counselling, Berne's theories have been used in education, communication training, management development, and organisational analysis.

Social factors

A major influence on communication research during the 1960s and 1970s was the rise of the protest movement. Public marches and sit-ins became powerful communication symbols in themselves. Consequently, the research of communication theorists focused less on how arguments were constructed, and more on aspects of communication such as persuasion and non-verbal behaviour. Similarly, television, film and popular music, once seen merely as entertainment, were now viewed by communication researchers as representations of, and a crucial impact on, popular culture.

From the 1960s and 1970s, to the present

During the 1960s and 1970s, there was a clear shift from a focus on the 'what' to a focus on the 'how'. Communication relationships became almost as important as the message itself; this echoed Laswell's highlighting of the importance of the effect of communication. Mirroring the growing interest in interpersonal skills, interest in media studies research developed rapidly, and related courses blossomed in many colleges and universities.

Theorist	Key Concept
Aristotle	Personal character, logicl analysis and emotional appeal are crucial elements in persuasion
Lasswell	An effect must be achieved for communication to be successful
Shannon & Weaver	'Noise' can be a significant barrier to effective communication
Osgood & Schramm	Shared experience makes successful communication more likely
Berlo	Successful communication means considering all the factors relating to source, message, channel and receiver
Harry Stack Sullivan	Personality can only be known and understood through the medium of interpersonsl skills
Wm. Schutz	All humans possess three key needs: the need for inclusion, the need for control and the need for affection
Eric Berne	Used the analogy of 'games' (social interactions) to develop an understanding of how people behave towards each other

Figure 9: A summary of the key communication theorists.

In terms of communication research, the decades from the 1960s and 1970s to the present can be seen to be aligned around a number of key issues:

- A move away from a focus on aspects of interpersonal studies such as group dynamics, non-verbal behaviour and persuasion, to a concentration on personal relationships and power relationships
- A focus on the cultural aspects of communication
- An emphasis on how messages are interpreted by individuals and groups
- An investigation into the cognitive processes that influence communication behaviour

However, it is important to remember, that although some researchers have changed their focus, aspects of interpersonal skills such as non-verbal skills, group dynamics and persuasion remain extremely important for many people in their day-to-day business and social interactions.

Summary

- Although the various communication models differ to a greater or lesser degree, they can be seen to lie within three main categories: the *technological*, the *psychological* and the *social-cultural*
- The Shannon-Weaver model focuses on a single message flowing in one direction, with the emphasis on transmission rather than effect
- Psychological models focus on the behaviour of individuals as message filters, rather than other channels. An example in this respect is the Osgood and Schramm model, because it is based on the view that individuals process information independently
- Social-cultural models combine both communication theory and psychology since they are based on the notion that communication occurs through social interaction. Important elements here are the concepts of shared meaning and that messages are the outcome of negotiation
- The field of communication studies incorporates both scientific and humanistic views of the world. One way of accommodating both views is to see communication as the management of messages for the purpose of creating meaning and understanding
- Whilst there is strength when a research discipline like communication studies has such many and varied themes, there is also an inherent weakness in the fact that no one is quite sure what the aim of the discipline really is. In other words, there seems to be no unifying vision
- Despite the negative aspects, communication theorists have developed various models that help us make sense of the wide range of communicating behaviour. Such models enable us to consider *why* we communicate, *what* we communicate, *how* we communicate and the *impact* of our communication on others. These factors are particularly important where business communication is concerned

Tutorial

1. Before you give the next important talk, consider the following:
   – what signals do you wish to send to others concerning your character? (ethos)
   – examine the points you wish to make, are they logical? (logos)
   – in what ways can you relate to the audience? (pathos)
   *A camcorder is useful for this
2. Using rhetorical devices such as anaphora or syllogism (review pages 2–4), develop an advertising slogan for a product or service.
3. Identify a key strategy you wish to implement, and using the principle of eristics (page 4), assess the arguments for and against.
4. Develop your powers of perception and analysis by reviewing and comparing three different newspapers. Using the modified questions relating to Laswell (page 7), determine the following:
   – do certain reports/'messages' differ? (If so, how)
   – do the newspapers favour/support any political view?
   – how might the above results affect business advertisers?
5. In what ways might a team leader or manager meet their staff needs for affection, inclusion and control? (review pages 9 and 10)
6. Using an organisation with which you are familiar, indicate what theoretical model of communication best describes its communication practices. Consider what improvements could be made to make its communication system more effective.

2 Communication and organisations

One-minute overview

Some organisations will purchase expensive information management systems and think that the organisation's communication problems are solved. Others focus on the external image, and believe that this, too, is the solution. The wise organisation, however, knows that the differences between information and communication include the important concepts of meaning, quality, purpose and appropriate methods. Wise organisations also realise the value of the people dimension of communication, and that what happens internally has a significant influence on how the organisation is perceived externally. Optimising the business means optimising communication in terms of developing suitable strategies, considering how all aspects of information and communication can be effectively deployed, and regularly evaluating and improving the system.

This chapter will enable you to:

- Understand the relationship between organisational culture, structure and communication
- Appreciate the impact of informal communication on organisations
- Recognise the importance of using information effectively
- Audit and improve communication systems

2.1 The importance of organisational communication

Communication is central to the success of organisations, and as figure 10 illustrates, it can be viewed in general terms such as planning and co-ordinating; organisational communication can also be seen in terms of specific communication methods like informing and persuading. The overall purpose of communication, in its various aspects, is to align employees with the organisation's strategic vision, and enable them to achieve their specific objectives.

Organisations cannot survive without planning for current and future work processes and events. The overall corporate strategy (e.g., 'to be the brand leader within three years') is broken down into a number of key objectives that can be applied to particular areas of the organisation (e.g. product or service, financial, marketing, human resources).

In turn, these broader objectives are guided and regulated by a series of controls such as policies, procedures and rules. Work-based problems can arise, and these have to be solved and related decisions made. One way of looking at the link between these organisational issues and communication is to see the function of communication as being *goal-related* or *task-related*.

Organisational Issues	Examples

Planning
Co-ordination
Control
Problem-solving
& Decision-making
Motivation
 	
Innovation & change
	– Goal-setting and forecasting
	– Monitoring the work of individuals, teams and processes
	– Setting and maintaining deadlines; resource management
	– Analysing work-based problems and arriving at the
	   best solution in the circumstances
	– Treating employees with respect, giving feedback
	   constructively, and involving employees in decisions
	– Communicating openly and positively to employees and
	   encouraging new ideas and practices

Figure 10: Organisational issues and examples of communication.

However, organisations cannot survive solely on technical know-how, work-based excellence or current reputation. It is the 'human factor' that gives most organisations the competitive edge. Accordingly, communication that is linked to issues like performance management, motivation and morale, and how the company is performing, is vital for the management of change and increased innovation. Sensibly handled, issues such as these can lead to increased job satisfaction, better integration between work groups, easier acceptance of change and greater innovation. The net result of these is improved employee relations, improved performance and superior organisational achievement. These aspects can be viewed in terms of *growth* or *innovative* organisational communication.

Regardless of the type or nature of the particular organisation, five key questions need to be answered with respect to organisational communication:

- **What needs to be communicated?**   (key messages)
- **Who will communicate it?**   (senders)
- **When should it be communicated?**   (timing)
- **To whom should it be communicated?**   (receivers)
- **How should it be communicated?**   (methods)

Although the above criteria are quite straightforward, it is surprising how often organisations get one or more of the criteria wrong. Whilst there can be simple explanations for communication problems within organisations—such as pressure of time, or choosing the wrong method—more often than not, it is factors such as culture, organisational structure, the values of the founders or owners and lack of a communications policy that have a fundamental impact on the very nature of an organisation's internal and external communications.

2.2 Organisational culture

Culture can be seen as the personality of the organisation, and is composed of factors like core beliefs, traditions and shared values. As the management guru Charles Handy has stated, 'It's the way we do things around here'. Peters and Waterman (*In Search of Excellence*) refer to the dominance and coherence of culture as being an essential feature of excellent companies. Culture has a significant influence on the behaviour of managers and other employees in terms of behaviour, how they communicate, and how they perceive and respond to events. Some issues in this respect are:

- What is acceptable/unacceptable
- Underlying assumptions about how issues are dealt with
- What behaviour is encouraged/discouraged
- How employees relate to management and each other (and vice versa)

Values are the bedrock of culture and are communicated to each generation of employees through mechanisms like mission statements, the role-modelling behaviour of senior management, stories, company legends and slogans (along with other strategies, the car rental company Avis helped close the gap with the then market leader Hertz, by using the slogan, '*We try harder because we're number two*'). Activities such as recruitment and selection, induction and appraisals also play their part in the communication and consolidation of values. Organisational culture is crucial for:

- Communicating and reinforcing the organisation's values and mission
- Forming a sense of identity and loyalty
- Creating and maintaining morale and motivation
- Securing commitment to key aims and objectives
- Offsetting the impact of key competitors
- Generating a positive working environment (e.g., diversity)
- Adapting to change

Although an organisation's culture can appear to be unusual or strange to outsiders, its value lies in its 'internal consistency'. An organisational culture will be strong and internally consistent when it sets clear expectations for all employees in terms of behaviour and conformity to organisational values. Whilst it has been explained above, that an organisation's culture is transmitted from one generation of employees to another, at the same time, it is also a dynamic and evolving process. This quality is vital if the organisation is to adapt to new business environments and challenges.

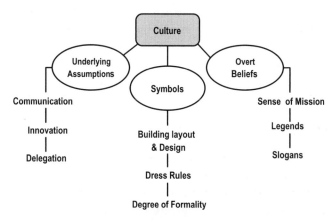

Figure 11: Aspects of organisational culture.

It is possible for sub-cultures to arise in organisations, and very often, these can have a beneficial effect. In most cases, such sub-cultures will be tolerated as long as they do not pose a threat to the dominant culture.

One crucial process that reflects the particular organisational culture is communication. For example, organisations that place a value on power, status, and rules and regulations tend to have a *closed* communication system. Here, information is disseminated on a need to know basis; those not in the know feel alienated and not trusted. Disagreement is not tolerated, and the dominant message is that 'management knows best'. Overall, a climate of 'them and us' develops that is quite damaging to the organisation.

Conversely, organisations that adapt a culture which values and emphasises relationships, tend to have an *open* communication system that underpins all organisational processes. Open communication is exemplified by the view that everyone has a right to information, that communication is everyone's business, and that people should have the right to disagree. In cultures that foster open communication, feedback is encouraged and the downward communication route is not the dominant one. Such cultures have additional advantages:

- Increased job satisfaction
- Greater ability to solve problems
- Improved quality and innovation
- Lower labour turnover

An organisation that promotes an open communication culture respects an employee's right to receive information about matters that affect them, respects their right to ask questions, gives them the freedom to share information and values their feedback.

2.3 Organisational structure

"My co-authors and I downplayed the importance of structure in *In Search of Excellence*, and again, in *A Passion of Excellence*. We were terribly mistaken."

Tom Peters

"Good organisational structure does not by itself produce good performance. However, a poor Organisational structure Makes good performance impossible."

Peter Drucker

As management writers such as Peters and Drucker confirm, organisational structure is a key element in organisational performance; but so, too, is communication. An examination of organisational structures will reveal that certain structures can be seen to facilitate good communication and, conversely, that other forms of structures inhibit communication behaviour that is crucial for good performance.

A number of factors have to be considered when determining the structure of an organisation. For instance:

- The type of activity (e.g., manufacturing)
- Aims and objectives
- The personal values of the founders/owners
- The degree of specialisation
- The size, type and number of departments (e.g. finance, marketing, personnel)
- Whether it is product- or people-intensive
- Technology

Whilst all the above factors have to be considered, the views and values of the key players and the purpose and goals of the enterprise will have a significant bearing on the final structure. In a way, structure and organisational culture have a sort of mutual cause and effect relationship; cultural values will have a bearing on structure, and, similarly, the structure will be a determining factor in the dominant culture that evolves. For example, tall pyramidal structures tend to create a culture that emphasises rules, regulations and downward communication; cultures that emphasise human relationships will tend to have flatter structures or a structure that is based on projects or teamwork.

Writing at the turn of the 20th century, Max Weber, a German philosopher and theorist, identified what he called the *Bureaucratic* organisation. Such organisations were governed by an extensive and binding system of rules, a hierarchical pattern of management, and decisions were based mainly on technical advice. In addition, the rules and decisions were always recorded in writing, and the control of staff was purely impersonal. Although such procedures meant that Bureaucratic organisations were reasonably efficient and fair to all workers, the downside was that initiative was discouraged, decisions took longer (thus, they were slow to react to change), and compliance with rules could become an end in itself.

In addition, the very long chain of command meant that communication not only took longer, but could often be distorted as it made its way down the hierarchy. Furthermore, the emphasis on 'paper communication' meant that interpersonal relationships and the associated skills were not harnessed in the interests of the organisation.

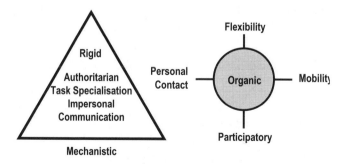

Figure 12: Characteristics of mechanistic and organic organisations.

Working in the 1960s, the British researchers Tom Burns and George Stalker studied twenty industrial firms in the UK. Their findings identified two different types of organisational structure: the *mechanistic* and the *organic*. Figure 12 illustrates that the mechanistic organisation resembled the Bureaucratic type previously identified by Weber in many respects. On the other hand, the organic structure was not only more flexible in design, but also flexible in terms of job specification, work roles, management style and attitudes towards people. Whilst the organic organisation did have levels, these tended to be based not only on seniority, but expertise. Because job roles were not as fixed as in the mechanistic organisation, there was greater mobility within the organic system. This led to increased participation between individuals and groups. Importantly, relationships in the organic organisation were mainly based on commitment and co-operation, rather than the competitive nature and preoccupation with performance of the mechanistic organisation.

The communication ramifications of the structural aspects of organisations are clear. Hierarchical structures exemplified by Weber's bureaucratic model, and Burns and Stalker's mechanistic model, tend to have communication processes that: are largely written, time-consuming, and that downplay the importance of interpersonal skills. On the other hand, organisational structures such as the organic encourage the free exchange of information and communication. Importantly, the very nature of their structure means that organic organisations encourage personal relationships and lateral communication; the communication content is largely based on advice, information and agreement (as opposed to the forms of direction and orders that personify hierarchical organisations). Whilst conflict is a feature of all organisations at times, the structure of hierarchical organisations means that conflict is largely resolved by superiors; in the organic organisation, it tends to be resolved through personal interaction and discussion by the people involved. All of these factors mean that organic organisations usually produce greater innovation and faster responses to changing conditions.

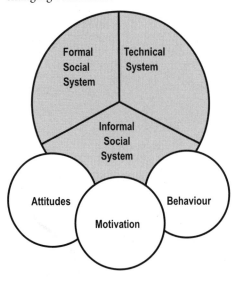

Figure 13: The socio-technical systems.

A view of organisations that combines the need for various levels, and a recognition of the importance of both technology and people, is the Socio-Technical System. As indicated by figure 13, whilst the importance of the formal social system within the organisational model is recognised, so also is the crucial part that the social element plays. No matter how good the technology is, or how efficient the formal social structure is in terms of co-ordination and control, superior organisational results are produced through people who are well motivated, behave positively to each other, and are suitably rewarded.

Seeing an organisation in terms of a socio-technical system means that the vital part communication plays in forming attitudes, informing behaviour and maintaining motivation is acknowledged. In turn, the potential impact of informal aspects such as the grapevine (see page 21) is appreciated, and appropriate steps can be taken to minimise any negative consequences. In addition, upward communication is encouraged and regular briefings conducted to stop any communication gaps from occurring.

2.4 The Management of information

Communication routes

Well-run organisations will have clear lines of communication. In many respects, these communication lines or routes represent the formal structure itself, and are key vehicles for conveying information relating to issues such as delegation of authority, directives, policies and work instructions. Communication routes take a number of different forms; the key routes being the *vertical* (i.e., downward through the organisational hierarchy; upward through the chain of command) and the *lateral* (e.g., from colleague to colleague, or department to department).

The downward vertical route is the main channel for management. communication. Whether the downward route from top management is the dominant one in an organisation depends upon various factors like organisational structure, the culture of the organisation and management style. An over-reliance on downward information flow can be reflective of an organisation that is overly bureaucratic, and where innovation and change will be more difficult to implement.

The upward flow of information along the vertical route constitutes accountability, but information is also gained about issues such as the reporting of results, problems encountered and the degree of work progress. Upward flows also play an important part in co-ordinating individuals, teams and departments. However, perceptive senior managers will always work on the principle that '*each of us is not as smart as all of us*'. Consequently, upward flows of information will be actively encouraged, and constructive responses made by management.

Lateral communication routes link people who work at similar levels in the organisation. Such communication occurs

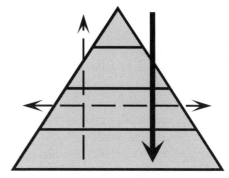

Figure 14: Communication routes in a hierarchical organisation.

throughout organisations, and in most cases, is a valuable source of the organisation's efficiency. In addition, it fosters positive interpersonal relations. Sometimes, a form of *diagonal* communication occurs when employees may have to deal with colleagues who are senior to them. This communication route is often discouraged by organisations that adopt an hierarchical structure, since it is deemed to undermine the chain of command.

Whatever the communication route adopted, organisational communication often suffers from the problem of *management filtering*. This is the process whereby middle management, for a variety of reasons, alters the original message in some way. This can be done for several reasons; for example, in a positive way, to prevent information overload (page 23), or in a more negative sense, to increase the power of a particular manager (knowledge is power). On occasions, filtering occurs to such an extent (or initial feedback is ignored) that employees are left with only extreme means of 'upward flow', such as high absenteeism, high labour turnover, or industrial action.

Informal communication

Regardless of how appropriate the fit is between factors such as culture and structure for particular organisations, other elements like informal communication can have a significant effect on organisations. As many have found to their cost, informal communication can be so powerful, that it undermines the formal, 'official message'. The basis of informal organisational communication is usually the *grapevine* (gossip, rumours or stories). Apart from the content of the 'message', additional alarming features of the grapevine for organisations are speed and exaggeration. For example, the consideration of a generous voluntary redundancy package for a few individuals on Monday can be transformed by the grapevine to compulsory redundancies for hundreds by Friday.

Informal routes of organisational communication such as the grapevine assume importance for a variety of reasons:

- The organisation fails to communicate
- Conflict between individuals
- Employee insecurity caused by issues such as change
- Some individuals just like causing problems for others

On one hand, then, the grapevine can be the result of understandable anxieties and fears resulting from organisational change or performance. On the other, it can be the product of malice or jealousy (e.g., a perceived personal slight, or resentment when someone gets promoted). Whatever the cause, organisations ignore it at their peril because it cannot be turned off, it has a high degree of credibility, it spreads rapidly and it can seriously damage organisations.

Sometimes organisations themselves cause the grapevine to flourish, by creating a communication gap or vacuum. However, it is not unknown for management themselves to use the grapevine when it will lead to a desired outcome. Despite the negative aspects of the grapevine, it has some redeeming features: it indicates that formal communication is not working; it acts as a safety valve when organisational stress intensifies; it can lead to a sense of belonging (recipients are 'in the know'); and it can act as a valuable source of feedback on particular work issues.

The grapevine is best defeated by management:

- Constantly keeping employees informed about events
- Holding briefings about specific initiatives
- Encouraging upward communication
- Listening and responding to any fears or anxieties

Using information effectively

The relationship between information and business has undergone fundamental change, and there are a number of reasons for this. Firstly, the bargaining power of customers has increased markedly; secondly, competition has greatly intensified; thirdly, the threat of substitute products has become a reality for many organisations; fourthly, many business organisations now operate in a global market place. Consequently, the management of information has assumed greater strategic significance for many organisations. In order to meet the challenges posed by this situation, customer orientation has become one of the critical activities for perceptive business organisations.

Being customer orientated entails obtaining information about the following:

– The size of the market
– Demand patterns
– Market structure
– Buying habits
– Market share
– Trend analysis (past and future)

Generally, consumers will tend to buy from companies who can provide the best combination of product, price and service. Therefore, one vital information factor for a company is knowledge of customer purchasing criteria. Sometimes, such key information factors can be generated through innovative means. One example here is when one UK supermarket introduced 'loyalty cards'. When they did, they were immediately accused of employing gimmicks by other retailers. However, the magnetic strip on the card was logging vital customer buying behaviour. This innovative corporate strategy was consolidated by the fact that the reward points offered acted as an incentive for the customer to repeat his or her buying behaviour. This is also an example of how a business can meet 'external' information requirements (customer buying behaviour) through internal means (IT solutions). The loyalty card illustration is also evidence of how a company can meet information demands in such a way that it gives them, relative to competitors, a key competitive advantage.

Just as factors such as operations, marketing and service are important elements of the value chain, it could be argued that, because of the business situation outlined above, information management has now become an important aspect of the value chain.

Figure 15: The demanding customer.

'Knowledge management' is the term given to the process where the collective skills, expertise, and knowledge of an organisation are identified, documented and utilised in order to achieve competitive advantage. Here again, the management of information can be seen to be a critical factor.

Important strategic information processes can be seen to form the circular pattern illustrated in figure 16. The first part of the process is *information demand*. Crucial information here will be that relating to customer, competitor and market place. The second part of the loop is the method of acquiring the information indicated by information demand. Here, existing internal and external sources need to be analysed for any gap, and a strategy devised to remedy the situation. The third aspect of the strategic information loop is the actual internal storage of the information generated. Fourthly and finally, is the process of information use. Since all of these elements are equally critical, great care must be taken to maximise the strategic advantage that could be extracted from the overall process.

Indeed, one of the current problems that seems to affect some business organisations, is that they tend to adopt a systems approach to information (i.e., a focus on technology), rather than viewing information as a necessary strategic resource (and therefore maximising its business impact). Despite this, even when some businesses realise the strategic value of information, its collection and storage, more often than not, has been driven by an emphasis on the system rather than its business use.

> **Mini Glossary**
>
> **Value Chain:** The collection of activities used to design, produce, market, deliver and support a product. Michael Porter, the originator of the theory, held that competitive advantage is gained when the value created, exceeds the cost of creating it

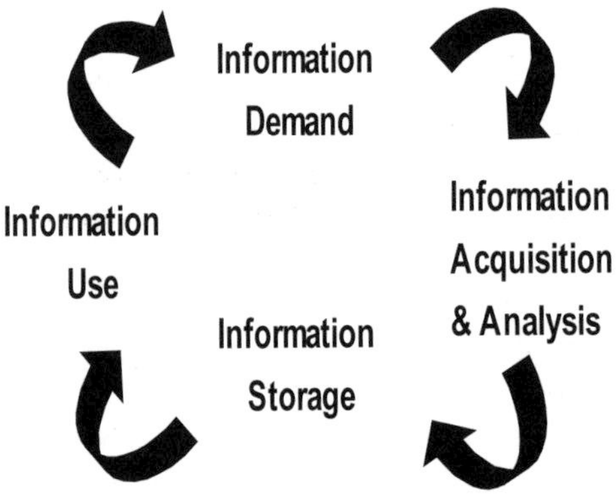

Information Demand

Information Acquisition & Analysis

Information Storage

Information Use

Figure 16: The Strategic information cycle.

For example, a survey by Accenture Information Management Services of more than 1,000 US and UK managers examined the way in which they gathered, analysed and used information. The survey found that the managers spent up to 25% of their time looking for the information they needed to do their jobs; when they did find it, over 50% found that the information was of little or no value to them. However, even finding the information was problematic. Of the managers surveyed, 60% stated that they had difficulty in finding information that could be useful to them.

Improving information management

The Accenture investigation is only one example of a growing body of research that highlights the problem of information overload. Modern computer-driven information systems have led to organisations being faced with an avalanche of information.

In addition to stress, coping with this avalanche has led to problems such as poor decision-making, time and other resources not being used effectively, and less than optimum business performance.

A number of strategies can be adopted that might limit the negative impact of information overload:

- Using technical information filters that ignore unwanted details
- Changing the information culture
- Training for all staff so that they can better recognise quality information

The key to optimising the strategic dimension of information is to integrate the generation of *relevant* information with the business process of the organisation. The '5WH' approach might be useful here:

What information do we need? (corporate objectives)
Where will it be stored? (issues of systems and accessibility)
When will it be used? (business timelines)
How will it be used? (securing competitive advantage)
Who are the key people? (strategic information managers/users)

Generating quality information means identifying information that helps meet the corporate objectives of the organisation; focusing on information that leads to a competitive advantage; and using internal and external systems effectively. Maximising quality information also means:

- Ensuring the right volume
- Having a central system (but linked to individual business areas)
- Ensuring easy access
- Screening and appropriate selection
- Getting the purpose right
- Using it effectively

Organisations also need to ensure that the information used internally and externally is accurate and cost effective. Because of the complicated nature of information in organisations, it is better to see it in terms of *specific usage, quality* and *effect.*

2.5 Auditing and improving the system

The communication audit

A communication audit is a systematic and comprehensive analysis of an organisation's internal or external communication. An audit provides management with important information about a range of issues associated with the overall communication process of the organisation. But audits do not just provide details about the communication system alone, they can also reveal significant information relating to the organisation's culture, structure, management communication style, how well the communication system is aligned with corporate objectives, the state of key initiatives and the overall image of the organisation.

Where the communication system itself is concerned, audits can reveal important details about issues like:

- The amount of information flowing through the system
- The quality of information flowing through the system
- The sources and destinations of key information
- The effectiveness of particular communication methods
- Informal aspects of communication
- Attitudes towards the existing communication process
- Any barriers to effective communication
- Any particular areas of concern
- Communication patterns (e.g., between individuals and groups)
- The nature and quality of communication relationships (e.g., the degree of trust, mutual support and job satisfaction)

Whilst some organisations conduct audits in conjunction with specific events such as the implementation of change, re-structuring, the launch of a new product or service or a crisis, the perceptive organisation will conduct communication audits on a regular basis (just as it would with financial elements). Again, these can focus on the entire organisation, or focus on particular departments or employee groups. Between special, extensive audits every few years, feedback on key communication areas can be gained by using the organisation's existing system (allowing for any deficiencies).

As to who will conduct the audit, there are advantages and disadvantages with regard to whether the organisation will use its own staff or bring in a consultant. Using internal staff who have received special training in conducting audits has the advantage that the person(s) has intimate knowledge of the organisation and how it functions. The disadvantage here is that the person may be 'blinkered' where certain problems are concerned, and the audit lacks objectivity. Conversely, apart from cost, the external consultant will lack important knowledge of how the organisation works in practice. However, external consultants can bring valuable attributes such as objectivity, experience, credibility and knowledge of current good practice.

A variety of methods can be used to conduct an audit, and these include: questionnaires, interviews, focus groups, log sheets and analysis of critical incidents. Each of these methods has its own specific value, and which one will be used depends upon the particular situation. For example, interviews can generate the important elements of meaning and a greater depth of response; additional, uninvited but valuable evidence can also be forthcoming. The investigation of a critical incident can be conducted as part of the questionnaire or interview process, or can be conducted in its own right. For instance, where there has been a serious failure in customer care, key questions might include: *what* actually occurred (the facts), *how* did this occur (the sequence of events), *when* did this occur (key dates and times), *who* was involved (key players). Through a process such as this, the communication auditor will be trying to establish what was ineffective in terms of communication behaviour, and how incidents like this might be remedied or avoided in the future. The methods outlined are not mutually exclusive, and more than one method may be used during a particular audit period. Whilst organisations and consultants may want to design their own audit instrument(s), the International Communication Audit (ICA) is a tried and tested method.

Usually, the audit process begins with a planning meeting to determine issues like: key aims and objectives, areas to be audited, the overall approach and a schedule of activities. The actual audit normally starts by conducting interviews with senior executives. This is because communication should be driven from the top; the top management also has its views on what the communication process should be achieving. An added dimension here is the identification of any communication problems at this level, along with impressions of the executive's communicating style. It is also the practice to interview the heads of the key functional areas along with those responsible for organisational communications.

The next step in the process is the collection and analysis of evidence relating to all aspects of the organisational

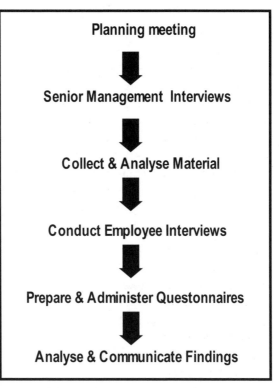

Figure 17: Stages in the audit process.

communication process. If relevant, external aspects of the organisation's communication process such as publicity, marketing material and its public image will also be examined. These need to be compared and assessed against the organisational needs that are formally expressed, and cross-matched with the evidence obtained from the questionnaire and the interview process.

Employee Interviews in the form of focus groups are an important element of the audit process. It is vital to have a good mix of employee types, in terms of age, experience and gender. In addition, it is also good practice to separate key figures such as supervisors or team leaders from the focus group, so that employees feel free to comment on sensitive issues. The issues raised by the focus groups can be explored in more depth by individual interviews.

The responses to the information gained from the above processes are vital to the questionnaire design process. Piloting (testing) the questionnaire on a small representative group first is recommended, since even well designed questionnaires can contain flaws. Administering the questionnaire and analysing the findings are the final stages in the audit process before communicating the results to the organisation.

Improving the system

Although what has been written so far in this chapter relates directly or indirectly to improving the communication system of organisations, there are a number of simple but effective strategies that organisations can adopt that will enhance their internal communications. Firstly, senior management must accept its responsibility for ensuring that the organisation has an effective communication system; in short, the lead must come from the top. Secondly, communication principles must be enshrined in a policy; the policy should stress:

- That good communication is vital to the success of the organisation
- That good communication is everyone's business
- The importance of an open communication climate
- The importance of upward flow and employee feedback
- The management's responsibility for creating and maintaining effective communication processes
- The importance of communication skills training

A third factor in the improvement of organisational communication is the identification and removal of any barriers. These can include:

- Lack of clarity with respect to job roles and related information
- Unclear levels of authority
- Poor personal communication style
- Lack of trust
- Too many levels (communication is diluted or misinterpreted as it moves through the system)
- The wrong communication method being used (e.g., a memo instead of face-to-face)
- Lack of information concerning key initiatives

Some of the barriers outlined above can be overcome by providing quality information relating to job specifications and roles; keeping the number of structural levels to a minimum; giving appropriate feedback on personal communication effectiveness; operating an open communication climate (page 18); conducting employee briefing sessions; and providing the means for employee feedback. Establishing suggestion schemes, grievance procedures and providing regular communication training are also vital strategies for overcoming the organisational barriers to effective communication.

Figure 18: The Personal information needs of the employee.

Focusing on the employee as an individual and considering their personal information needs is another key aspect of improving an organisation's communication climate. Details about issues like job functions, the degree and scope of responsibilities, specific work information, how their performance will be judged, and how their career is going to be managed are key requirements in terms of personal, work—related information. So, too, is information about processes related to how problems might be resolved. Important aspects here are details relating to grievance and disciplinary issues. It is also essential to provide employees with information relating to the overall state of the organisation, its projected performance and any issues that may affect this. The organisation that is not afraid to deal with negative information is much better placed to have an impact on its consequences.

Viewing employees in the wider sense, in terms of how the organisation relates to them as a group, is also vitally important. Though corporate communication methods such as in-house magazines sometimes score low ratings in research, they can be seen to perform important functions such as maintaining morale and providing a sense of identity (particularly during tough times). 'Good news' stories such as 'employee of the month' and 'best performing branch' bring recognition for effort and engender a feeling of camaraderie and common purpose. Similarly, news about proposed projects or initiatives, promotions and new personnel, convey messages of success and security. Most importantly, in-house magazines provide an essential source of employee feedback on a range of issues.

The pressures of the modern organisational environment often lead to a common fault that can have serious ramifications—the mismatch between communication method and purpose. Some of the most common methods of internal organisational communication are often the most ineffective. For instance, research indicates that notice boards are a relatively ineffective means of communicating to employees, whilst team briefings consistently score very highly. There are several reasons for this: notice boards are a one-way method of communication, there is no guarantee that the message has been received and understood, they become part of the organisational 'scenery' (low impact), the messages are often out of date. Conversely, although team briefings are a one-way method, they contain the important element of face-to-face contact.

To avoid the problems of communication method mismatch, it is useful for key groups such as managers to see communication methods in three main ways: as relating to levels or areas in the organisation, as forming an 'hierarchy of communication effectiveness', and in terms of the advantages and disadvantages of each method. The first

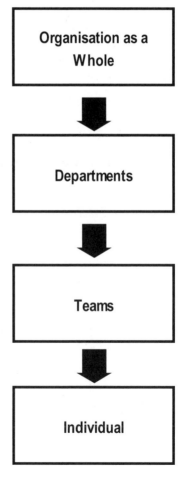

Figure 19: Levels of communication (receivers).

two of these categories are illustrated in figures 19 and 20, and the advantages and disadvantages of each method are detailed below.

The *face-to-face method* (level one) has clear advantages such as the value of personal contact itself, reinforcement through non-verbal communication and feedback. However, it requires more time than other methods, there can often be no detailed record, and inappropriate words, misinterpretations, and lack of clarity can occur.

Level two methods such as the telephone have advantages like convenience, interaction and immediate feedback. Disadvantages include inappropriate timing on occasions, difficulty in terminating the conversation, and less impact than face-to-face methods.

One-way methods are at the bottom level in terms of overall impact. By their nature, they lack interaction and can be seen as impersonal. Furthermore, feedback is delayed, and the words used can present problems at times. On the plus side, level three communication methods can be better planned, have a better structure, provide a record and can be widely distributed.

For many organisations, maximising the business means maximising communication. As the content of this section indicates, this can be best achieved by adopting a strategic approach. Such an approach entails optimising intelligence about customers, competitors and the market; encouraging a positive and open communication climate internally; projecting a positive external image; ensuring that all the quality information generated meets corporate objectives; monitoring organisational communication regularly; identifying information and communication needs, and matching these appropriately (e.g., the correct volume of information and using the correct method). Another crucial activity is conducting regular training.

Just as communication has entered the value chain as one of the critical factors in organisations achieving and maintaining competitive advantage, organisations themselves have undergone significant and fundamental change. Indeed, through the use of modern communications techniques, it is possible for some organisations to assume structures never before thought achievable—the virtual organisation is now a reality.

However, the vast majority of working people (whether as executives, managers, or general employees) find themselves operating within highly structured and highly complex organisations; and the common bond that unites them all is communication.

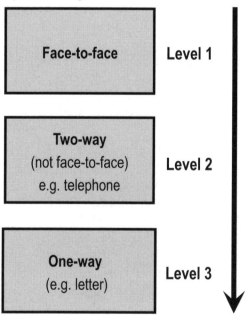

Figure 20: Levels of communication (methods).

Accordingly, organisational communication is not just a means of securing corporate objectives, market prominence or profit maximisation. Properly conceived and executed, communication within an organisational context develops and maximises not just the organisation, but the individual. It unites workers in an interpersonal (face-to-face) or other relational sense; it unites them in a job specific sense, and it gives them an important sense of identity and common purpose.

Summary

- The overall purpose of organisational communication is to align employees with the organisation's strategic vision and enable them to achieve their specific work objectives
- Five key questions need to be answered with respect to organisational communication:
  - What needs to be communicated?   (key messages)
  - Who will communicate it?   (senders)
  - When should it be communicated?   (timing)
  - To whom should it be communicated? (receivers)
  - How should it be communicated?   (methods)
- The culture of an organisation can be seen as its 'personality', and is composed of factors like core beliefs, traditions and shared values. Culture has a significant impact on communication activities by reinforcing the organisation's values and mission, forming a sense of identity and loyalty, and generating a positive working environment
- The particular structural form adopted by an organisation can facilitate or hinder communication
- The power of informal communication (such as the 'grapevine') should never be underestimated
- The key to optimising the strategic dimension of organisational information is to integrate the generation of relevant in formation with the business process. Key questions here are: what information do we need? where will it be stored? how will it be used?
- Information management in particular, and organisation communication in general, can be improved by:
  - technical information filters
  - changing the information culture
  - staff training
  - focusing on the employee as an individual
  - considering the personal and job information needs of employees
- A communications audit provides management with important information about a range of issues that include: the communication system itself; the culture of the organisation and its structure; communication styles; and the degree to which the communication system is aligned with corporate objectives
- Problems of communication methods mismatch can be avoided by viewing communication methods as relating to levels in an organisation; as forming a

hierarchy of communication effectiveness; and in terms of the advantages and disadvantages of each method

- Organisational communication is not just a means of securing corporate objectives, market prominence, or profit maximisation. Properly conceived and executed, organisational communication develops the individual as well as the organisation

Tutorial

Using an organisation you have access to, try and determine the following:

1. a. What its culture is (e.g. dress, degree of formality etc.)
   b. What structure does the organisation adopt? (e.g. hierarchical)
   c. How does a and b above affect its internal communication climate?
2. What evidence can you find of a grapevine; how does informal communication affect employee relations?
3. The key market and customer information the organisation needs to achieve competitive advantage
4. How the organisation's management of information and general communication system might be improved (e.g. is there a communication strategy or policy? could it be enhanced?)

3 Maximising yourself 1

One-minute overview

Whilst seeing a gap in the market or having an innovative idea still has an important place in modern business, the days of simply developing a product or service and hoping for success are largely gone. Modern businesses prosper on intuitively understanding customer needs and buying behaviour, and meeting these successfully. Understanding those we work with is also essential for discharging the obligation to customers or clients. Consequently, perceptively understanding others is a key business attribute. But just understanding others is not enough; the essence of business, the human dimension, is only fully realised by understanding yourself as well. Accordingly, maximising the business means maximising yourself in terms of developing an understanding of who you are, what motivates you, how you are likely to react in certain situations, how others might perceive you and identifying self development.

This chapter will enable you to:

- Appreciate the importance of self-awareness
- Understand the significance of personality types
- Be aware of how others may perceive you
- Realise the value of emotional intelligence
- Engage in self-development
- Understand the learning process

3.1 Intrapersonal intelligence

Who looks outside, dreams; who looks inside, awakens

Carl Jung

A fundamental factor that influences our behaviour towards others is our ability to understand what shapes us as a person; aspects such as our general self-awareness, personal emotions and how we see the world (and our place in it). The name given to this important process that affects our communication with others is *intrapersonal* intelligence.

People who have good intrapersonal intelligence are aware of their inner processes and thinking to a degree that they know their strengths and weaknesses and can interpret a range of behaviour from others (and respond appropriately). Intrapersonal intelligence enables us to make sense of the things that we do, the emotions and feelings that we have, and how to manage these. In short, intrapersonal intelligence provides the tools for effective self-management and interpersonal skills.

Intrapersonal intelligence, then, is a process consisting of *self-awareness, social awareness, self management*, and *self development*. The premise is simple, if we cannot manage ourselves effectively, we will have difficulty in working with or managing others, and successfully executing the interpersonal processes that are necessary for personal and professional success.

Having a strong intrapersonal intelligence enables one to determine:

- What our values are
- What motivates us
- What our personal goals are
- How we respond emotionally to certain events
- How others might perceive us
- What our strong points are
- What personal areas need developing
- How we solve problems
- How we learn
- How confident we are
- The degree to which others trust us

Intrapersonal intelligence enables us to be introspective in a positive way, to analyse our thoughts, feelings and actions with a view to personal and professional improvement. This generation of self-knowledge provides a clearer vision of who we are and where we want to go; it enables us to have more control over events, and not just react to them. These are critical factors for personal and business success.

Figure 21: Intrapersonal intelligence.

We can develop our self-awareness in a number of ways. For example, by analysing our personality, values, opinions, attitudes and any stereotypes we may have; by evaluating how we tend to act in various situations (particularly those that test us emotionally or ethically); by reflecting on how we relate to others in an interpersonal sense; and by receiving feedback from those whose opinions we value.

It is understandable that some people take the view that our personality tends to be fixed, and, therefore, there is no real value in trying to alter what is a large and dominant feature of who we are as individuals. If this were the case, then one's personal and professional life would simply become a self-fulfilling prophecy. Yes, behavioural change is difficult, but increasing our self-knowledge can bring about an awareness of those elements of our character that need to be modified. Often, even a small improvement in people's behaviour can make the difference between success and failure at the job interview, a project being accepted and the much-desired promotion being achieved. A key aspect of who we are and how we behave is our personality.

Personality

Our personality is an important aspect of our self-image, it reflects who we are and how we perceive the world. By its very nature, personality is a very complex matter, and can be seen to be composed of various elements such as traits and one's emotional state at any given moment. A *trait* can be described as a relatively enduring or permanent individual characteristic, such as being outgoing, friendly or shy. Conversely, a *state* is a temporary change to one's personality. To complicate the issue further, there are occasions when a trait can also be a state, and vice versa. One way forward here is to view how the person *typically* reacts (a trait), and how they might be reacting, in a *temporary* sense, to a particular event (a state). For instance, a normally confident (trait) businessperson might become anxious or even depressed (a state) when an important aspect of a new project is not going to plan.

Whilst the sometimes heated debate continues as to whether traits are inherited ('nature') or are acquired by our experiences of the world at critical stages (e.g., when we are quite young—the 'nurture' argument), it is not unreasonable to assume that one can inherit certain traits from our parents (e.g., the gift of music or other ability or a skill). Similarly, a supreme human quality is that we are capable of learning from experience. It is important in a personal and a business sense, that one is not sidetracked by theoretical debates about whether traits are inherited or acquired from experience, but to explore every opportunity to optimise one's knowledge, skills, abilities and behaviour.

As mentioned at the outset, how we relate to others in a personal sense is vitally linked to business success. Consequently, it is important to examine our personality in order to determine how we might be perceived by others. Unfortunately, there are as many theories of personality as there are aspects to it. Indeed, sources such as the internet abound with personality tests; many of these are self-administered. For any test to have a significant value, they need to be administered and interpreted by trained staff. Even then, and as figure 22 indicates, it must be remembered that *where* an individual may be on the particular characteristic scale depends on a number of factors (such as the particular situation). Therefore, personality tests only indicate *tendencies* to act in a certain manner. Nevertheless, it is also fair to say that individuals can have dominant traits.

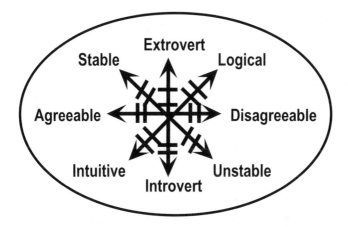

Figure 22: Some dimensions of personality.

Even within this context, however, it is important not to stereotype; just because a person may have a tendency to be disagreeable, for instance, does not mean they do not have compensating features. Many people who tend not to agree about a range of issues that others may accept may simply be displaying their dominant characteristic of challenging the status quo or 'accepted truths' (for hundreds of years, most people thought the world was flat!).

Such individuals can be very innovative and inventive and often make excellent entrepreneurs. Many of the significant changes in business, commerce and the world, in general, were brought about by people who challenged the accepted truths of the day.

Whilst it is also good to have people in the business team who are agreeable, the downside here is that they may be so eager to agree with others, they may not be able to take an objective view of a proposal or new initiative. Accordingly, they may not be able to spot problems; or when they do so, be unwilling to speak out.

As with any of the traits shown in figure 22, extroversion has both positive and negative aspects. On the positive side, extroverts tend to think positively, enjoy being with people and engage with the world around them; such individuals make excellent team members. Despite these positive traits, extroverts can persistently seek the limelight and may not wish to listen to the views of others. That is why it is crucial for team leaders or colleagues to moderate the behaviour of extroverts and seek the views of team members who tend not to express them.

Although being introverted can be a sign that the individual lacks the 'get up and go' that is so necessary for success in business and life in general, it is important to note that people who tend to be introverted, can have positive traits such as excellent listening skills. They can often have a considered view of an issue or problem that more outgoing team members may lack.

Positive and negative points can be made about any personality trait; the key point is that one should seek to get an objective view about what our dominant personality traits are, and identify any negative points (and how these can be moderated). Although this may involve seeking help from professionals who specialise in psychometric testing, significant results can also be achieved by adopting a common sense approach. Such an approach can involve seeking the views of close friends and work colleagues.

Whilst it is difficult to arrive at an objective view of your personality, asking yourself some key questions is also a way forward:

- How would I describe myself?
- How might others describe me?
- How do I relate to others generally?
- What are my positive personality traits?
- What are my negative personality traits?
- How do I tend to react to certain situations (e.g. those I don't like)?
- What is my communicating style?
- Is any behaviour detracting from my business performance?

One way of addressing the first two questions is to use the *Johari Window*. Developed by Joseph Luft and Harry Ingham, the Johari Window is designed to elicit information in two main respects: what we know about ourselves, and what others know about us. Figure 23 represents four main panes of the window: the Open area, the Hidden

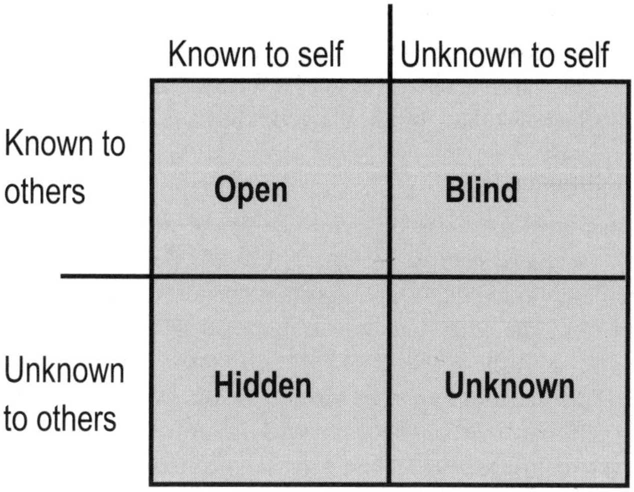

	Known to self	Unknown to self
Known to others	Open	Blind
Unknown to others	Hidden	Unknown

Figure 23: The Johari window.

area, the Blind area and the Unknown area. The Open area represents the information about us that is known to others. When the relationship is new, the known window is quite small. However, the more one reveals about oneself, the bigger the window grows. The Hidden area concerns information we know about ourselves, but is hidden from others. If the person is more revealing and/or begins to trust others, the Hidden area reduces. The Blind area contains information that others are aware of, but the individual is not. This situation can be changed through feedback from others (the Hidden area reduces and the open area increases).

Finally, the Unknown area represents information that is unknown to us and others. This situation is mainly due to a lack of knowledge regarding how individuals might behave in certain circumstances; for example, someone who is giving a business presentation to a large audience for the first time. The Unknown area can also contain information that has genuinely been forgotten or purposely suppressed. As one grows and develops, the Hidden area can become smaller. It is important to remember that personal growth is largely a process of self-discovery; self-awareness allows us to assimilate experiences, learn from them and move forward as a person.

The above processes can often be painful, since our view of ourselves can often be at odds with the views that others have of us. Generating the evidence can also entail revealing details that one might prefer to keep private; this is the reason why one should only involve those we trust implicitly. Once the information is gained, the next step in the process is to decide how we are going to respond. It may be that only minor modifications need to be made in the way we relate to others and respond to certain events. Even if this is the case, some sort of action plan will be required. Where more fundamental change is required concerning one's dominant traits, interpersonal skills training may well be necessary.

As mentioned earlier, our dominant personality traits tend to be fixed. But this does not mean that they cannot be modified; developing an awareness of what aspects of our personality we need to change is, in itself the first step in the behaviour modification process. For example, if a person can improve their listening skills by

20%, they are 20% better than they were before; if a person learns to maintain eye contact during interviews and meetings, that's a significant improvement on their previous performance; if a person learns to be less critical and more constructive, they will not only maximise business performance, but be a better person.

Emotional intelligence (EI)

Whilst emotional intelligence can be seen to be similar to intrapersonal intelligence in many ways, it is treated here as a component of intrapersonal intelligence. This is because of the desire to highlight the important area of human emotions as related to, but distinct from, the other areas of intrapersonal skills. The popular interest in EI can be seen to lie in the success of Dr. Daniel Goleman's 1995 book, *Emotional Intelligence* (an international bestseller within two years). Another indicator of the interest in EI was the fact that, when the Harvard Business Review published an article about EI in 2005, it attracted the highest percentage of readers than any other article in the previous forty years. However, the 1990 journal article of psychologists Peter Salovey and John Mayer (*Emotional Intelligence*), and the pioneering 1930s work of Edward Thorndike (who coined the term, 'social intelligence') were also significant contributions to the field of EI.

EI is a way of recognising, understanding and controlling how we think, feel and act. It affects not only how we understand our own emotions, but how we respond to the emotions of others. Even if some EI research is inaccurate (such as the piece of American research that indicated that EI is responsible for 80% of our success in life), there is little doubt that our ability to manage our emotions and our managed response to the emotions of others is a critical factor in personal and business success.

There are four important aspects to EI:

- Knowing and understanding your emotions
- Managing your emotions in a variety of contexts
- Recognising and understanding the emotions of others
- Managing the emotions of others (i.e. managing relationships)

The ability to be empathetic, to be 'tuned-in' to the emotions of others through the ability to 'read' verbal and non-verbal cues, is, for many people, much easier than trying to recognise our own emotions and how we are likely to act in certain circumstances.

Emotions convey information, and how we interpret and react to information related to people, circumstances and events is a significant factor in our emotional response. A key aspect here is to differentiate and re-prioritise between thinking, feeling and doing.

Being emotionally perceptive enables us to consider the most appropriate way to react to experiences that might upset us, or hinder our ability to optimise a particular business

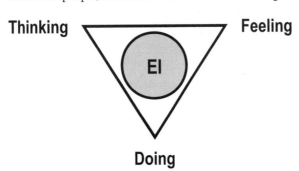

Figure 24: Being emotionally perceptive.

response. For example, if one takes the situation where a customer criticises the way they *feel* they have been treated:

Interaction A

Customer: "Your customer care is appalling"!

Business person's response (feels attacked): "Don't raise your voice, we have done our best"

Customer: "You're talking rubbish" etc.

Interaction B

Customer: "Your customer care is appalling"!

Business person's response:

Thinking mode: (I need to keep this customer—and the shop is full)

Feeling (empathy) mode: "I can see you're upset, please calm down so I can help you ... what exactly happened?"

Doing mode: "I am sorry you feel you have had a bad experience on this occasion. I will knock 10% off this bill and 10% of your next order. If you have any further problems, contact me personally, here's my direct telephone number"

Although understandable, the business person's response in interaction A has three main outcomes: firstly, it becomes part of a downward spiral of negative emotions; secondly, it could lose the company a valuable customer (and perhaps others); thirdly, both parties will be upset and angry. Where interaction B is concerned, the business person not only exercised emotional empathy ("I can see you're upset..."), but also emotional self control. Emotional self-control is the ability to exercise some sort of restraint where our feelings and emotions are concerned—for example, the ability to deal with work stress constructively, not to respond negatively to provocation, and to calmly resolve conflict from others when it does arise.

Overall, interaction B demonstrated the business person's ability to be emotionally intelligent (as well as being practical). Being emotionally intelligent entails:

- Improving our ability to read and interpret emotions
- Being able to express our feelings ("you're making me feel guilty by saying...")
- Distinguishing between thoughts, feelings and actions (as outlined above)
- Controlling our desire to make immediate emotional responses
- Taking more responsibility for our emotions ("I'm feeling angry"; rather than, "you're making me angry")

Accordingly, EI can be seen as a type of social intelligence that involves a perceptive understanding of how we think, feel and act. Properly harnessed, it can lead to a better understanding of ourselves and others, improved interaction with others, and enhanced intuitive decision-making (the 'gut' reaction).

Self-management

As confirmed by the comments about EI, there is a strong link between elements of EI and self-management. However, self-management is a more general process that entails effectively responding to all the aspects of self knowledge we have gained through the process of self awareness. Self-management involves regulating those feelings, thoughts and attitudes that may hinder positive relationships with others; being accountable for our actions; responding appropriately to problems and stressful situations; setting and maintaining clear goals and objectives. Self-management is also about being positive, conscientious, dependable, honest and determined to succeed. Individuals who are self managed tend to be:

- Highly focused
- Results orientated
- Well balanced
- Successful
- Sound role models

3.2 Self-development

Self-development is taking responsibility for one's personal growth and career development; it is a process that follows on from the activities outlined in section 3.1. It involves being motivated, identifying any learning needs, being focused and setting goals. Self-development also means being open to new ideas and new methods, being willing to learn from others, and seeking and receiving feedback. Learning from failure and recovering from setbacks is another crucial aspect.

From a skills point of view, there is a high correlation between personal development and career development. For example, acquiring the skills of learning in an individual sense will also have a positive impact on developing learning in a work setting. Similarly, developing skills such as problem solving, decision-making, relationship management and change management will have a beneficial impact in the personal and work context. No matter how many skills we develop, we will never be able to use them effectively, unless we are really motivated.

Motivation

Motivation can be described as a driving force within individuals to achieve some goal, fulfil a need, or meet an expectation. It can also be said that a person's behaviour is strongly influenced by what motivates them. In a work setting, a person's performance is largely determined not just by motivation, but by factors such as ability. Motivation is a highly complex affair, with aspects such as needs and expectations, values, relationships, economic aspects and feedback from others coming into play. Additional factors like inherited dispositions, life experiences and social factors also have an impact on an individual's motivation.

Having a balanced set of values is vital for motivation. For example, research has shown that, while factors like salary, and working conditions are important, these alone are not enough to develop or maintain high motivation. Some theorists argue that, in order for motivation to be maximised, intrinsic aspects of work such as a sense of achievement, being challenged, enhanced responsibility or recognition are also necessary.

Maintaining motivation means: clarifying your personal and career objectives, having a balanced set of values, adopting a positive attitude, setting realistic and achievable targets and being aware of potential threats to your motivation.

The Self-development plan (SDP)

Although a degree of self-development can occur without planning, a plan not only speeds up the process, but provides better focus and increases the likelihood of the plan being realised. The existence of a plan also means that the individual is not merely reacting to events, but is being proactive and determined to achieve the set goals. Moreover, a self-development plan provides milestones that are critical for creating and maintaining motivation.

Very often, there can be a strong link between personal and work goals. For example, the desire to make the most of a skill, ability or interest that gives a person a lot of enjoyment might be realised by developing a career in a field that requires the particular skill, ability or interest. However, as figure 25 indicates, sometimes compromises have to be made between extrinsic motivators such as a high salary, with intrinsic motivators like the pleasure derived from doing the job itself.

The first step in the SDP process is identifying what needs to be developed in personal or work terms. In personal terms, this may involve a behavioural change or improvement. Where work is concerned, it could mean learning a new skill or managing change more effectively. Whatever the situation, a useful device is the SWOT process. This forces the person to think about their **s**trengths, **w**eaknesses, **o**pportunities and **t**hreats.

Figure 26 illustrates how the personal factors of confidence, capability and quietness may be seen in SWOT analysis terms. For example, a person who is seen as confident may be viewed in the strength area as not being daunted by new challenges.

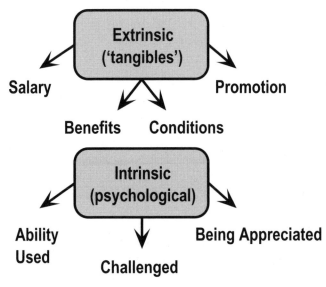

Figure 25: Two types of motivation.

Factor	Strengths	Weaknesses	Opportunities	Threats
Confident	Takes on new challenges	Might be seen as arrogant	Given more responsibility	May not be seen as a team player
Capable	Seen as reliable	Reluctant to delegate	Possible promotion	Others may resent them
Quiet	More reflective	Lacks impact	To become more assertive	May not be taken seriously

Figure 26: Example of a personal SWOT analysis.

However, a potential weakness is that they may be seen by some as being arrogant. Where opportunities are concerned, their confidence may result in being given new responsibilities. A possible threat is that they are not seen as a team player.

The SWOT analysis process (as applied to self-development) is important in a number of respects. It:

- Identifies the possession of key skills, and highlights new skills that may be required
- Provides a focus for current achievements
- Highlights desirable and undesirable behaviours
- Helps you focus on important learning opportunities
- Promotes continuous learning
- Helps you identify learning opportunities at work (and optimise these)
- Enables you to understand how you might be viewed by others

The SWOT analysis process also helps you set self-development goals; this is a vital part of the SDP. A second stage in the SWOT process is to link up the separate quadrants to help you form an action plan. For example, linking strengths and opportunities to form the SO quadrant enables you to focus on your strengths and develop strategies to exploit these to your advantage. Similarly, linking strengths with threats to form the ST quadrant assists in highlighting ways in which you can use your strengths to reduce or overcome threats to your self-development goals.

Joining weaknesses and opportunities to create the WO quadrant enables you to develop strategies to overcome your weaknesses; such a process can also help you identify ways of making your skills or abilities more effective. Lastly, in this second stage of the SWOT process, the WT quadrant is formed by joining the weakness and strength areas. Examining the WT quadrant helps you avoid threats that might arise from your weaknesses, or eliminate them altogether by turning weaknesses into strengths.

An overview of the four SWOT quadrants at stage two of the process will enable you to develop more effective goals and strategies to achieve them. The quadrants can be summarised as follows:

SO quadrant (Strengths combined with opportunities) ⇒ opportunities to pursue

ST quadrant (strengths combined with threats) ⇒ threats to eliminate

WO quadrant (weaknesses combined with opportunities) ⇒ things to improve

WT quadrant (weaknesses combined with threats) ⇒ minimising and avoiding threats

Goal-setting

Goal-setting is an important part of deciding what is important in your personal and working life. It is also an important source of self-confidence, since it is linked to the achievement of key objectives. Consequently, goal-setting creates long-term vision and short-term motivation. Not all goals will be achieved, but failure to realise goals must be offset against lessons learned. Common problems associated with goal-setting include having too many goals, failure to prioritise goals and lack of goal clarity (see figure 27).

Deciding what goals to set for yourself is not an easy task, and is best attempted by focusing on *why* you have set the goal, and what attaining the desired goal requires in terms of attitude, or skills, or behaviour. The attainment of goals is also influenced by considering *when* the goal is to be achieved, and the best method of achieving it (the *how*). Therefore, when writing goal statements, all of these factors should be borne in mind. Goal clarity is paramount, and the following are examples of weak and strong goals:

Vague goal	Clear goal
To improve my interpersonal skills	When communicating, I need to listen carefully and consider non-verbal, as well as verbal behaviour
To be more assertive	I need to choose the outcome I want, and maintain firm eye contact and body posture. I also need to use a confident tone of voice

Figure 27: Setting clear goals.

Since goal-setting is about identifying and achieving personal and work-related objectives, it is important that the goals be realistic and achievable. Goals will also need to be monitored and evaluated to ensure that the level of expectation can be adjusted (upwards, if improvements are made, downwards, if they are set too high).

Using an incremental approach to goal-setting is important for developing confidence; so too is setting timelines. Whilst small goals can be reached in a relatively short time, larger or more complicated goals can take much longer. In addition, it is vital that goals have a degree of flexibility built-in to allow for unforeseen circumstances.

As a rule of thumb, set two to five years for medium range goals, and five years and beyond for long-term goals. Adopting an incremental approach to goal-setting (e.g., eighteen months broken down into six month cycles) will make the goal more manageable and improve self confidence when each stage is reached).

As the 'SMART' acronym indicates, goals should be:

Specific – As figure 27 verifies, setting clear goals is crucial for focus, direction and purpose.

Measurable – Clear goal definitions and a description of the desired outcome will help you to monitor and measure goal attainment.

Attainable – Nothing will undermine confidence and motivation more than setting goals that have little chance of being achieved. (either in terms of time, task difficulty, or lack of ability)

Realistic – As indicated in 'attainable' above, goals need to be set that stretch your skills and abilities, but at the same time, are possible to achieve. Realism also applies in terms of timelines and other aspects that must be within your control.

Time-related – Setting deadlines provides targets to reach, and is an important part of the action plan. Setting deadlines also helps create a momentum for change, and is vital for confidence-building when the goal is reached. Matching goals with time targets is also important for planning the sequence of self-development.

Learning for development

Self-development will invariably involve some sort of learning process, and whether it occurs in a work or other setting, learning lies at the heart of the self-development process. Whilst formal, off-the-job learning may be necessary, it may be the case that some self-development goals can be achieved through informal, on-the-job training. The value of informal, self-directed learning in the workplace is not to be under estimated, since it occurs in a much wider variety of settings than formal learning. But it is not just variety in terms of settings, variety where the 'how' of learning is concerned is vitally important: working as a member of a team; working alongside experienced individuals; working with clients; tackling tasks that stretch one's knowledge, skills and abilities. Self-directed learning is also particularly effective because it accommodates the individual's objectives and learning style.

How one reaches self-directed learning goals is affected by a number of factors, including the learning opportunity itself, learning factors such as those in figure 28, the skills of learning (figure 29) and, as mentioned above, learning style (figure 30).

Understanding – An active mental process that enables us to put together information in such a way that it helps us to make sense of ideas, concepts, theories etc

| General Learning Factors | Acquiring knowledge Transferring knowledge Evaluating what we have learned | Understanding Memorising Doing | Specific Learning Factors |

Figure 28:

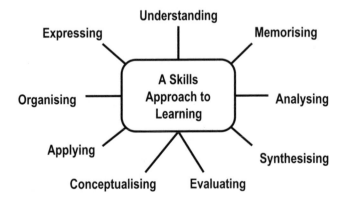

Understanding

Expressing

Memorising

Organising — A Skills Approach to Learning — Analysing

Applying

Synthesising

Conceptualising   Evaluating

Figure 29:

Memorising – Retaining and recalling information

Analysing – Arriving at an understanding by examining the individual parts of a topic, theory, task or problem ('breaking things down')

Synthesising – Arriving at an understanding through examining the larger structure ('putting it together')

Evaluating – Making a value judgement

Conceptualising – Linking or classifying particular items of information or knowledge to create an overall idea or meaningful whole (generalising from particular examples)

Applying – Putting theory into practice ('doing it')

Organising – Putting things into a logical, efficient and effective order

Expressing – Presenting information clearly, concisely and logically; both verbally and in writing

The term 'learning style' describes a person's particular approach to learning; their preferred attitudes, behaviour and activities concerning the learning process. Styles are usually the result of our learning behaviour; through experience, we realise which particular learning strategies are successful for us.

The terms used to describe various learning styles differ. Here, the categories of 'enthusiastic', 'imaginative', 'practical' and 'logical' represent the different styles. Using these as examples, individuals preferring the enthusiastic style would tend to be impulsive and accept ideas readily; those opting for the imaginative style take time to consider and evaluate new ideas and experiences.

It is important to remember that move than one style may be used during a particular learning event.

Learning Style	Positive	Negative
Enthusiastic	Works quickly Works intuitively Tries new ideas Reads quickly	Little advance planning Attempts too many tasks Important details missed Not selective with notes
Imaginative	Innovative thinker Takes time Links study areas Interesting formats	Poor time management Accepts ideas too readily Slow to get started Easily distracted
Practical	Sets goals Can apply theory Researches well Meets deadlines	Can lack imagination Can fail to see links Pre-occupied with details Prefers own ideas
Logical	Good critical powers Organises well Precise & thorough Prioritises work	Led mainly by logic Tends to be uncreative Can get lost in theory Needs a lot of information

Figure 30:

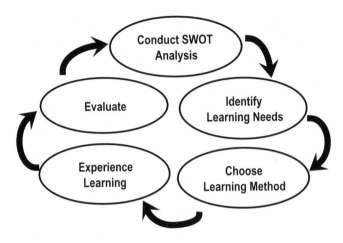

Figure 31: The self development learning process.

As figure 29 illustrates, adopting a skills approach to learning is important for making the most of the learning opportunity; so, too, is the process of evaluation. Key questions need to be asked here:

- To what extent did the learning event meet my development goals?
- Could I have learned more from the event?
- What can I now do better as a result?
- Can I transfer the learning to other areas?
- Have I identified further learning needs?

Learning in pursuit of self-development goals can be optimised by adopting a number of strategies: being proactive in seeking work-related training courses and other learning opportunities, identifying role models from whom you can learn, seeking and acting on feedback, and building a learning network inside and outside the workplace. In addition, not all learning opportunities will be successful; it is important to be able to cope with failure and negative feedback. It is also useful to keep a 'learning log' so that learning experiences can be reflected upon; this is valuable for motivation and measuring progress.

Continual learning is an essential part of developing yourself as a person as well as a business professional. The more we understand ourselves, the more we might be able to understand others. Learning about yourself and others and enhancing personal and professional skills is the foundation of good business practice; in maximising ourselves, we maximise the business.

Summary

- Intrapersonal intelligence enables us to be introspective in a positive way; to analyse our thoughts, feelings and actions with a view to personal and professional improvement
- Our personality is an important aspect of our self-image, it reflects who we are and how we perceive the world

- Emotional intelligence is the ability to recognise, understand and control how we think, feel and act. It affects not only how we understand our own emotions, but also how we understand and respond to the emotions of others
- Self-management involves regulating those feelings, thoughts and attitudes that may hinder positive relationships with others; responding appropriately to problems and stressful situations; setting and maintaining clear goals and values
- Self-development is taking responsibility for one's personal growth and career development. It also means being open to new ideas, and being willing to learn from others
- A self-development plan speeds up the development process, provides better focus, and increases the likelihood of the plan being realised. A useful device here is the SWOT analysis process
- Motivation can be described as a driving force within individuals to achieve some goal, fulfil a need, or meet an expectation. Motivation is a highly complex affair, with aspects such as needs and expectations, values, relationships, economic matters and feedback from others coming into play
- Learning in pursuit of self-development goals can be optimised by adopting a number of strategies:
  - being proactive in seeking work-related training courses and other learning opportunities
  - identifying role models from whom you can learn
  - seeking and acting on feedback
  - building a learning network inside and outside the workplace

Tutorial

1. Who am I?
   a. List ten words that describe who you are
   b. List ten words that describe how others might see you
   c. Identify any differences between the above; how might these impact upon the way you communicate with others?

2. Being emotionally intelligent
   a. Recall a personal or a professional situation that you found emotionally stressful. Using the *thinking, feeling* and *doing* dimensions of emotional intelligence, assess how you might have minimised the impact on yourself
   b. Using the whole section on emotional intelligence as a basis, develop a personal strategy that will enable you to be more emotionally perceptive in the way you communicate

3. My values are…
   a. Write down your six key values and prioritise these. What does this tell you about yourself? In what ways might these values affect what you do, how you do it and your overall communication style?
   b. Determine the extent to which your current job meets the various aspects of intrinsic and extrinsic reward. In what ways does any perceived imbalance affect your motivation? In what ways might you unconsciously communicate this?

4. Using SWOT analysis
   a. Using the SWOT model outline on pages 37 and 38, create a self-development plan. As part of this plan, set and prioritise clear SMART goals
   b. In connection with the above plan, identify any learning needs you may have, and how these can be met

4 Maximising yourself 2

One-minute overview

Communication research confirms that competence in interpersonal skills is a significant factor in personal and business success. Competency in interpersonal skills entails an awareness of the impact of non-verbal behaviour on our communication with others, clarity of oral communication, careful choice of language, identifying our main communication style and adapting its use to different situations. Maximising yourself in business terms also means competency in the skills of persuasion, negotiation, questioning, listening and giving or receiving feedback.

This chapter will enable you to:

- Understand the need for good interpersonal skills
- Develop an awareness of particular aspects of interpersonal skills like non-verbal communication and communication style
- Appreciate the importance of negotiation elements such as planning, identifying interests, bargaining, problem solving and language
- Improve your ability to question, listen and give and receive feedback

4.1 The importance of interpersonal skills

Powerful as they are, words alone are not enough to ensure effective communication. Whilst the percentages may differ, communication research confirms that a significant degree of personal and work success depends upon our interpersonal skills. It is the possession of such skills that enable us to communicate and reinforce our ideas, beliefs, values and feelings.

However, interpersonal communication is more than the mere encoding, transmission and decoding of a particular 'message'; it involves a whole range of learned behaviours that are goal-directed, and appropriate to the specific situation. People who possess good interpersonal skills:

- Effectively manage their behaviour during social interactions
- Understand and positively manage the emotions and behaviour of others
- Are sensitive to the needs of others and can empathise with them
- Can project a positive image of themselves and their organisation
- Can work effectively with others in a variety of situations (e.g., teamwork)

Presenting ourselves effectively entails proficiency in a whole range of communicative behaviour such as using signs of recognition and approval, signalling our agreement/disagreement, empathising with others and responding effectively to them. Key elements here are oral communication, paralanguage and non-verbal communication.

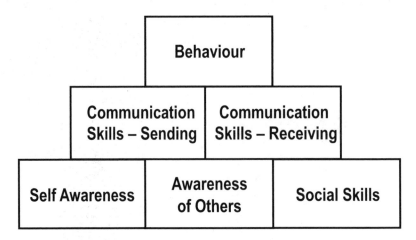

Figure 32: The Building blocks of interpersonal skills.

Oral communication

Whilst oral aspects of communication will be dealt with later in this chapter, it is worth mentioning, at this stage, the importance of matching the substance and style of speech and its supporting elements to the interpersonal situation. As indicated in chapter three, communication can be a very complex process at times; this is particularly so where oral communication is concerned.

For instance, oral communication can be enhanced or undermined by *paralanguage*.

Paralanguage can be expressed consciously or unconsciously, and is used to modify meaning or convey emotion. It is about how something is said, rather than what is said. For example, if someone says something with a sarcastic tone of voice, then the tone has more significance than the actual words.

Paralanguage entails aspects of speech such as volume, tone, emphasis, speed of delivery and personal vocal habits such as 'ah'.

By its very nature, communication is dynamic and, therefore: meanings are constructed in relation to various factors, meanings can change constantly, and meanings lie in people as well as words (e.g., the other person can select what they want to hear and 'reconstruct' the message). Because of these elements, it is crucial when communicating orally that:

- The message components are carefully selected
- The key points are stated clearly and precisely
- Simple language is used
- The appropriate tone is adopted
- The other person's communicating style is accommodated
- Checks for understanding are made
- Questions are asked
- Effective listening is demonstrated (e.g., good eye contact)

Non-verbal communication

Non-verbal communication is consciously or unconsciously conveying meaning through methods other than words. Such methods consist of: appearance, facial expressions, eye contact, proxemics ('personal space'; how we sit or stand in relation to others), gestures, touch and listening. Again, whilst research results in terms of percentages can vary, there is general agreement about the work of researchers such as Dr. Albert Mehabian.

Mehabian contended that, where face-to-face contact is concerned, only 7% of the meaning comes from the words used; 38% from the voice, and 55% from non-verbal behaviour. Other research indicates that, where verbal and non-verbal signals are not matched, people will tend to believe the non-verbal signals.

Whilst some aspects of non-verbal behaviour can be influenced by cultural and gender factors, there is still general agreement about many elements. For instance, smiling is generally accepted as indicating

Figure 33:

warmth, friendliness and the desire to be helpful. Conversely, poor eye contact can signal lack of interest, shyness, boredom or distrust. Similarly, raised eyebrows can communicate surprise; frowns can indicate disbelief or displeasure. Figure 33 illustrates the powerful impact that facial features in general, and the eyes in particular, can have on our non-verbal communication. It is no surprise that the eyes have been described as the 'mirror of the soul'.

Body positions can also be powerful indicators of mood. A person sitting or standing with arms folded across their chest ('closed posture') generally communicates anger, defensiveness or dislike. Body positions are also effective signals of rapport between individuals. Psychologists use the term 'mirroring' to describe the situation where individuals unconsciously copy each other's body positions when there is a high degree of rapport.

Different postures can communicate different non-verbal messages. Leaning forward, for instance, can signal that a person welcomes the presence, words or behaviour of another. Conversely, leaning backwards can convey the opposite message.

Figure 34: Posture & gesture signals.

Generally speaking, people tend to adopt 'closed' postures or positions (e.g., arms folded) when speaking to people they may not like. Importantly, in the business sense, whereas a good, straight posture indicates confidence, slouching can convey lack of confidence or uneasiness.

Hand gestures, recognised as an almost universal language, can be a strong aid to communication. Some cultures would almost be unable to communicate without them; they can convey a range of emotions from conviction and passion to anger and sadness. Nevertheless, in a business setting, especially a formal presentation, uncontrolled gestures can prove distracting and seriously undermine the 'message'.

Proxemics is how an individual uses space when communicating with another in an interpersonal sense. These informal spatial distances can be strong indicators of interpersonal behaviour. Researcher and writer Edward Hall denoted four space zones:

1. The *intimate zone* (from physical contact to eighteen inches)
2. The *personal zone* (from eighteen inches to four feet)
3. The *social zone* (from four to twelve feet)
4. The *public zone* (beyond twelve feet)

Spatial distances are particularly subject to gender and cultural influences. For example, although countries such as Japan have become 'Westernised', there are still Japanese and other cultures where business people tend to be more formal; this is often reflected in spatial distance and lack of overt behaviour. However, 'social distance' is not just determined by cultural influences. Many individuals, regardless of culture, prefer to 'keep their distance' until the relationship matures.

The immediate environment is also an important factor in interpersonal communication. For example, many interviewers prefer to leave their desks and sit closer to the interviewee. The rationale for this is that the desk can be seen as a barrier to communication; the closer the interviewer is to the person being interviewed, the better the rapport. Where there is a good rapport, the interviewee often discloses more about themselves. It is important to note that spatial zones can be 'crossed' quickly in certain cultures—the importance of the handshake in personal and business life should never be underestimated.

Our personal appearance, especially in a business setting, sends strong signals about not so much who we think we are, but who *others* think we are. Though many areas of business have become less formal where dress is concerned, it is useful to remember that dress is an important aspect of non-verbal communication. Whether we like it or not, dress is still seen by many in the business world as an indication of standards. The best advice where dress is concerned is to 'dress like them'. If it is not possible to ascertain how people dress in a particular organisation or setting, then it is best to dress formally (gents can always remove their jacket and tie, and ladies can remove a formal jacket).

4.2 Communication style

The preceding chapter examined factors such as personality, self-awareness and awareness of others; one critical element of personal communication that really sends strong signals about who we are and how we perceive others and events is our communication style. Communication style is the overall way we behave when we communicate with others. For instance, some individuals are quite loud when they communicate in an interpersonal sense, others are quite quiet; some take a long time getting to the point, others prefer brevity; some appear friendly, whilst others come across as quite cold and unfriendly. In many cases, it is not just the words that are used, but *how* they are used, and supporting features like sighs, tone of voice and non-verbal behaviour (e.g., smiles, frowns, eye contact and 'social distance').

One of the key business communication skills is the ability to converse with people from different backgrounds, cultures and level of education. A prime skill here is the ability to understand the range of communication styles, and to be able to adjust our own style accordingly. This is not a matter of changing who we are, but appreciating that people are different and express themselves in different ways. Learning to adapt your communicating style to the style of others can make the impact of our communication more effective. For example, if your style tends to be assertive/enthusiastic, and you are conversing with a colleague or customer who is quiet and reflective, it would be more effective if you slowed down delivery, asked questions and listened more.

There are many factors that influence communication style, but the principal ones are national culture, family environment and personality. Where national culture is concerned, most Westerners tend to prefer direct and explicit styles of communication. Conversely, other cultures (e.g., Asian) tend to prefer a more circular style where there is a high reliance on context, and the main point can be often be implied rather than stated.

Another additional factor here is emotion. Some races can be highly emotional and gesticulate quite a lot during ordinary conversation. One must be careful of stereotyping, however, and family environment can lead to variations. An example here is an individual growing up in a family with a largely quiet disposition; such a person will tend to have a quiet and reflective communication style.

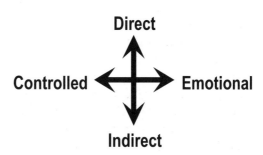

Figure 35: Aspects of communication style.

Nevertheless, human beings can respond and adapt to the many factors that influence communication style. Therefore, the most sensible way forward is to see *trends* in communication style with many influences contributing to these. One useful approach to communication style is to focus on three main types: passive, aggressive and assertive.

The *passive communication style* is often associated with lack of confidence and/or low self-esteem. It is largely based upon compliance and the avoidance of conflict. It often entails the individual putting the rights of others before their own. The passive individual mostly has a deferential manner and a soft, almost apologetic, voice. Non-verbal behaviour largely takes the form of lack of firm eye contact and a stooped posture.

Outcomes:
– Even lower self-esteem
– Self-anger
– Lack of respect from others

Individuals who use an *aggressive communication style* make their point and achieve their goals mainly by negating the rights of others. This type of communication style often involves manipulation or control of some sort. The verbal style of aggressors tends to take the form of 'you-type' statements, and a loud voice is often used. The non-verbal aspects of the aggressive communication style can range from stares and frowns to tense posture and invasion of personal space.

Outcomes:
- Anger from others
- Disrespect from others
- Resentment from others

Key aspects of the *assertive communication style* are: maintaining your rights whilst respecting the rights of others; the consideration that the other person has equal status; a firm voice accompanied by 'I' statements. Non-verbal elements of the assertive communication style include firm eye contact, supported by relaxed posture, gestures and movements. This is the communication style of a person who is confident and has high self-esteem.

Outcomes:
- Higher self-esteem
- Clearly understood by others
- Respected by others

The most effective communication style

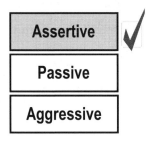

Figure 36: Types of communitin style.

Although perceptive communicators adjust their communication style to specific situations, the most effective style overall is assertiveness. This because it allows the communicator to:

- Maintain their rights without depriving others of theirs
- Handle awkward or difficult situations with confidence
- Disagree with others without causing offence
- Refuse to do something without causing resentment

Checklist—assertiveness involves ✓

- Listening carefully (what are they actually saying?)
- Recognising the views, opinions and rights of others
- Using an appropriate tone of voice
- Choosing your words carefully (avoid alienating them)
- Displaying appropriate behaviour (e.g., good eye contact, nodding etc.)

In short:

Practise active listening   (identify the issue, situation or problem)

Give your honest view   (the impact of the issue, situation or problem)

Convey the outcome you desire   (your view as to how the issue, situation or
                                                  problem might be resolved)

4.3 Persuasion

This section on persuasion deals mainly with persuasion in an interpersonal or small group context. Persuasion in general terms is a process that attempts to bring about change; usually in relation to behaviour, attitude, thoughts, or beliefs. In a business sense, it is a fundamental and legitimate activity that features in areas such as selling, marketing, advertising and public relations. In the increasingly non-hierarchical and democratic workplace of today, persuasion has become a vital skill that not just managers but everyone in the organisation needs to be proficient in. As with most skills, persuasion has an important transfer value in terms of one's personal life.

Ethical persuasion does not involve deceit or pressure, but relies on the use of evidence that is presented in a compelling and appropriate manner. This is crucial if the person to be persuaded is to make a decision that remains relevantly permanent. For example, pressuring a customer to buy a product or service they are basically unhappy with will not lead to repeat business. The central issue here is to realise that, although some aspects of persuasion such as advertising are largely one-way, effective persuasion in an interpersonal sense entails the element of participation—the attempt to persuade others is more likely to be successful if they feel that they have participated in the process (in modern terminology, 'buy-in'). The key skills associated with persuasion are:

- Active listening
- Empathy
- Identifying the needs of others
- Giving and receiving feedback
- Using evidence effectively
- Adapting your communication style
- Overcoming negativity
- Thinking creatively

However, the above skills alone are not enough; persuasion stands or falls on the perceived *credibility* of the persuader. Again, Aristotle's elements of ethos (credibility of the persuader), logos (the logic and interest of the argument) and pathos (the emotional connection) assume critical importance. Credibility can be seen to be composed of several elements: product knowledge or expertise; being confident and assured; trustworthiness; impression management and structuring.

Although trustworthiness is dealt with in detail on pages 85–88, simply stated, trust is the belief in the word, actions or decisions of another; and where required, the willingness to act on this belief. Impression management entails proficiency in the areas previously referred to in this chapter (interpersonal skills and communication style), and also areas of chapter three, such as personality and emotional intelligence.

Structuring is largely Aristotle's logos, and refers to the way the persuader plans the key elements of the message; and builds-in opportunities for the involvement of the person to be persuaded. Another important aspect of the structuring process is the composition of the message and its main constituents (the key selling points).

Aristotle's pathos, the emotional aspect of the persuasion framework, needs to be pursued sensitively. There must also be a careful balance between logic and emotion. If the person or group to be persuaded detects any notion of emotional manipulation, this will not only result in the persuasion process being unsuccessful, but could damage the reputation of the would-be persuader and their organisation. A classic example of making an emotional connection to a large audience in modern times was President Kennedy's simple, but hugely effective address to residents of Berlin. Kennedy made a strong emotional connection by using the words, "Eich bin ein Berliner" ("I am a Berliner").

Persuasion has a greater chance of being successful if it meets the following tests:

Appropriateness – the belief on the part of those to be persuaded, that the proposed action is the correct thing to do

Consistency – the degree to which the persuasion appeal conforms to the experiences, beliefs and values of the person/people to be persuaded

Effectiveness – the extent to which the proposed action leads to an outcome desired by the person/people to be persuaded (e.g., the advertising slogan, 'relief from pain')

The language of persuasion

The following are examples of the way in which elements of language are used to persuade:

Personal projection   e.g. the use of first names or personal pronouns ("Mike, this will…"; "*You* will…")

Active speech   e.g. "This *will* give your company the competitive edge"

Selective use of ideas   e.g. "This will meet not just your current, but your future needs as well"

Selective use of data   e.g. "This has captured 30% of the market already" (but rejected by 70%)

Short phrases/sentences   e.g. "This product is a winner already"

Use of adjectives/adverbs   e.g. latest, outstanding, leading (product), turnaround, world-beater

Use of emotion   e.g. 'starving children', "our only hope", "we are relying on you"

Implied urgency   e.g. "This special offer closes tomorrow"

Emphasis   e.g. "No maintenance required"

Overcoming objections   e.g. "Yes, it is *slightly* more expensive, but we can discount if…"

As stated previously, ethical business practice requires that persuasion does not involve manipulation, undue pressure, misleading statements, or deceit. Persuasion can be highly effective if you:

- Demonstrate trustworthiness
- Identify people's needs in a genuine way

- Are committed to your company, product or service
- Have confidence and demonstrate this
- Balance emotional appeal with logic and credibility
- Possess well-developed communication skills
- Can adjust your communication style

*How to persuade effectively in terms of oral presentations is discussed in chapter 5

4.4 Negotiation

Persuasion is an important component of negotiation, and some of the key skills are common to both areas. However, negotiation is different in that it is based on the notion that two or more parties have something the other wants, and there is an attempt to reach an agreement through bargaining. Thus, bargaining and compromise are the bedrock of negotiation; communication is central to the whole process. The key to successful negotiation is the willingness to compromise; trading something that is of less value to you at a particular point in time, in order to gain something else that is more valuable to you at a certain point in time. There are three main outcomes to negotiation:

Lose/lose – both sides cannot reach agreement and, therefore, there is no mutual gain

Win/lose – one side wins and, of course, the other loses; this can create a legacy of bitterness and discontent

Win/win – this is the most desirable outcome to negotiations; mutual gain

Types of negotiation

Distributive bargaining

Distributive bargaining is based on the premise of dividing or allocating a fixed amount of resources. An example in this respect, would be a buyer in an advantageous position who negotiates a price deal to the disadvantage of the seller. Distributive bargaining invariably produces an adversarial approach that leads to a win-lose situation (or lose-lose, if there is a failure to reach agreement). Since the strategy is on winning at the expense of the other, the emphasis is on the short, rather than the long-term. Distributive bargaining is appropriate in circumstances where the chance of a win-win outcome is unlikely; where the issue is urgent; when relationships are subordinate to the matter being discussed. It is important to note that the potential for conflict is mediated by the fact that both sides cannot entirely get their own way. Otherwise, they would not be negotiating in the first place.

Interest-based (integrative) bargaining

Whereas distributive bargaining is based on mutually exclusive positions, interest-based bargaining focuses on a more collaborative approach. Here, the parties feel there is a chance of individual goals being reached without each side 'losing'. Accordingly, the focus is on mutual interests rather than adversarial positions, and the intended outcome is win-win. Unlike distributive bargaining, interest-based bargaining places a high value on personal relationships, and requires key qualities and skills. The following comments in this section relate to interest-based bargaining.

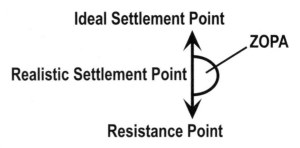

Figure 37: The range of possible resolution points.

Key negotiating terms

Position   The term position is associated with positional bargaining. This involves adopting a position (e.g., an ideal outcome) and defending it at all costs. Such an approach usually leads to conflict and deadlock

Interests   Interests are what the negotiator values or needs. Adopting the situation of positional bargaining outlined above often leads to interests being obscured or over-ridden

ZOPA   This stands for Zone Of Possible Agreement, and describes the identification of more than one resolution point (a range of options)

BATNA   Your BATNA is your Best Alternative To A Negotiated Agreement. In short, your 'plan B' if you are unable to continue negotiating (e.g., the other side is unwilling to compromise at all)

As figure 37 confirms, the Zone Of Possible Agreement is the range of potential resolution points that lie around the realistic settlement point. The range lies between both side's resistance point (their 'bottom line' that they will not be pushed beyond), and their ideal settlement point. Agreements within the range will call for compromise from both parties.

Information and communication

As mentioned previously, information and communication are central to the negotiation process. One of the best ways to illustrate this is to consider the information and communication aspects of each stage of the negotiation process. Addressing these aspects is vital if a successful outcome to negotiations is to be reached.

Planning and preparing

Doing your homework is vital for successful negotiation. Establishing key information at this stage entails asking key open-type questions such as the following:

Plan & Prepare

Clarify Procedure

Bargain & Problem-solve

Close & Implement

Figure 38: States of negotiation.

- What are the main issues for me/them?
- What are my/their interests?
- What is the relative importance of each issue? (for me and them—prioritise)
- What is my/their overall strategy? (e.g., what is my BATNA? what might be theirs?)
- Do I have enough information?

As indicated above, an important feature of planning and preparing is trying to ascertain information that applies to the other side. However, issues such as the other side's strategy might not be apparent until the negotiation begins. If this is the case, then skills like listening become critical.

Clarifying procedure

Some areas of negotiation like employment issues (e.g., management/trade union negotiations) have formal procedures that need to be followed. However, even if no formal procedures exist, it is good practice to set ground rules of some sort. Key information requirements at this stage include:

- What are the issues to be negotiated?
- Will issues be discussed in any order (an agenda is useful—potentially easier issues at the start)?
- Will there be a preliminary meeting(s)?
- How will conflict be resolved?
- What time will be allocated to the negotiations (what if you don't reach agreement in this period)?
- Will objective criteria be used to assess certain issues? (e.g., custom and practice, an outside expert)

Bargaining and problem solving

This stage of the negotiation process involves both parties communicating clearly and using information in creative ways in order to generate options. Seeking and maximising information leads to knowledge about what the other side really values; this is one of the key factors in successful negotiation. It would be unrealistic to expect both sides to divulge everything, and some issues may be addressed by using 'signalling behaviour'; this will be discussed in the section on 'the language of negotiation'.

Where communication during bargaining is concerned:

- Listen actively (what *exactly* are they saying)
- Clarify (so are you saying…?)
- Speak *to* the other side rather than debate issues
- Avoid emotional language
- Use language to build relationships and develop trust
- Use the KISS approach (Keep It Short & Simple)—keep your language and statements short and simple

Closing and implementing

Because the energy-sapping bargaining and problem solving stage is over, it is all too easy to see the final stage of closing and implementing as being less important; this would be a serious error. Genuine mistakes can occur over interpretations of key issues, and what has actually been agreed. Therefore, it is crucial to confirm verbally, issue by issue what has been agreed to, and written notes are invaluable. At the closing stage, it is imperative to:

- Clarify and confirm what has actually been agreed to
- Consider the short and long-term consequences
- Agree on any arrangements for implementation
- Draft and sign the agreement (both parties)

*A good agreement is when you get most of your needs and some of your wants

Some negotiation tactics

Even parties engaged in negotiations based on ethical behaviour can pursue a number of legitimate tactics. Examples in this respect are *making the pie bigger*, making *'yesable' proposals, compensating* and *re-packaging*. Making the pie bigger entails the creative use of a bargaining chip. Say, for instance, that an aid agency was trying to get food through a rebel roadblock in a war-torn country, and the only bargaining chip the agency had was friends in the media. During negotiations, the rebels indicated their need for media support in the forthcoming elections.

> ### The 'pie' = a media event
>
> **Slice 1: a photo opportunity (offer)**
>
> **Gain:** safe passage for the first aid convoy
>
> **Slice 2: a press conference (offer)**
>
> **Gain:** safe passage for another aid convoy
>
> **Slice 3: International TV coverage (offer)**
>
> **Gain:** more talks about future aid

Figure 39: Making the pie bigger.

Figure 39 shows how the lead negotiator for the aid agency maximised the offer of media support by 'making the pie bigger'. In other words, had the negotiator offered the international television coverage up front, all he would have gained would have been the safe passage for the one convoy. By composing the media offer of a photo shoot of the rebel leader helping to distribute the aid, then extending this to a press conference, and finally, international television coverage (and offering these at different times), he was able to gain safe passage for the first convoy, the agreement for another aid convoy, and the offer of more talks on aid issues. The aid agency negotiator was careful not to guarantee any media event, but simply to do his best to bring this about. Any negotiator who promises something when they are not certain they can deliver risks losing his or her credibility. For example, circumstances outside their control may mean that they cannot deliver what they have promised; such a situation also seriously undermines the important factor of trust. Language here is vital, and the negotiator should always use caveats; for instance, "I cannot guarantee this, but will do my best to bring it about."

Making *'yesable' proposals* consists of one side offering a concession that the other side will almost certainly accept. There are several problems here. Firstly, this could be interpreted as eagerness to reach an agreement at any cost; secondly and implicitly, this could be taken as a sign of weakness; thirdly, this may encourage the other side simply to wait for further concessions. Yesable proposals should only be used to move talks forward that are stalling, to test the goodwill of the other party, or to trigger the 'law of reciprocity' (I have scratched your back, now you must scratch mine). The timing of yesable proposals is crucial, and they should be at the bottom of the proposer's value range.

The *compensating tactic* is basically a 'swings and roundabouts' approach. It involves one side balancing what the other side perceives to be a loss. For instance, when one party points out that the other party's price is too high, a compensating response might be, "Yes, our prices on this particular product range are slightly higher, but the quality is much higher than other products on the market. If you order in bulk, we will discount." It is important to note that the compensator involves another gain for the seller, bulk orders. On the buyer's side, they will get a superior product—a win-win situation. Once again, the language used by the seller plays a vital role.

Re-packaging applies to both parties in a negotiation, and can involve substance as well as language. It is not unusual in business to delay payment, but this can prove problematic to sellers, especially if development costs have to be recouped. The following is an example of re-packaging:

Buyer: "OK, we will up this to 4,000 units now, with a first option for another 3,000, but the payment will have to be spread over twelve months"

Seller: "You know this is the best product of its type in the last five years, we have invested heavily in its development. We guarantee to supply to *you only* for the first six months, but we will need 60% of the payment up front, with the rest over four months"

Buyer: "If you can guarantee us sole supply for eight months it's a deal"

The above example is not just an illustration of re-packaging, but again, how a win-win situation can be developed. By simple re-packaging, the seller has gained an important customer for a new product with guaranteed sales. The seller has also managed to recoup some of his development costs. On the other hand, the buyer has gained a much-needed new product, and guaranteed sole supply for eight months; enough time to give them a substantial lead in the retail market.

The language of negotiation

The importance of language in negotiations should never be underestimated. In their classic work on negotiation, *Getting to Yes*, Roger Fisher and William Ury recount the incident in 1980 when the UN Secretary General Kurt Waldheim went to Iran to deal with the hostage crisis. Before formal negotiations began, the Iranian media repeated (in Persian) a remark that Waldheim had reportedly made on his arrival, "I have come as a *mediator* to work out a *compromise*"—Waldheim's car was stoned in the street. Whilst Waldheim's remarks appeared innocuous enough, the problem lay in the fact that some words mean different things to different people; especially in different cultures.

Apparently, in Persian, the word compromise has no direct positive translation. In Persian, the nearest meaning is a negative one, such as, 'her virtue was compromised', or, 'our integrity was compromised'. Things got worse for Waldheim; the word mediator in Persian means meddler.

Although some examples have already been given as to the general importance of language in negotiations, the following illustrations emphasise the importance of key words:

"We won't release *all* the hostages *now*" Here, the hostage-takers may be signalling two significant things; firstly, that they may be willing to release some of the hostages, and secondly, that all the hostages may be released at some point in the future

"*I* can't accept *these* conditions" This statement could indicate two things. That the other party would be willing to consider amended conditions, and that he or she may not have the authority to accept them (they may need to consult someone more senior)

"This is the best deal you will get" This statement, of course, could be true, but the other side could be merely stating their MSP (*their* Most Satisfactory Position). In other words, it's the best deal for them

Negotiations can be tiring, the other side may be difficult and the time period can stretch over many hours or even longer. In such circumstances, it is possible to lose one's cool and use language that may cost you dear or stop the negotiations altogether. As the following examples show, it is better not to be tempted to reveal your true thoughts. This is not being duplicitous, but merely the exercise of impression management skills and good negotiating practice.

Refrain from saying	Instead, perhaps
"Your deadline is ridiculous"	**"We want to help you, but It will take much longer to co-ordinate this amount of aid"**
"If you keep on insisting on these conditions, the talks will break down"	**"If we can't reach an agreement, all our hard work will be in vain, and I will be replaced by a senior executive"** This statement signals three things; firstly, that the other side's efforts are appreciated; secondly, the credit for any agreement could go to someone else; thirdly, that the senior executive will probably drive a much harder bargain. In addition, using the words 'break down' may actually create this very situation
"I've had enough of this going around in circles"	**"Let's have a break for now, and perhaps a drink. If you agree, we can start again in the morning"** Using words like those opposite, are emotional. They create disharmony; and in addition, they may bring about the end of the negotiations. Having a break not only lets things calm down, but gives valuable time for each side to consider a way forward (e.g., re-packaging proposals). The offer of a drink also signals that there is no personal animosity (goodwill is vital for successful negotiations)

Negotiating successfully means:

- Effective preparation
- Identifying and prioritising your interests
- Planning strategy and bargaining tactics
- Viewing negotiation as a series of stages
- Avoiding entrenched positions
- Thinking of the long-term as well as the short-term
- Planning for win-win outcomes
- Generating and optimising key information
- Listening effectively
- Communicating competently (e.g., using language carefully)
- Reading people effectively (e.g., non-verbal behaviour)
- Seeking and giving feedback
- Having a plan B (your BATNA)

4.5 Questioning, listening and giving feedback

Questioning

The fact that questions are such a frequent part of everyday life often means that their business value is underestimated. In fact, questions underpin a vast range of business activity, from colleague to colleague informal and formal communication, internal operations and client and customer contact, to externalising the product or service range of the company. In addition, customer care and after sales service are now critical factors in business success. These activities cannot be successfully discharged unless customer needs are identified; customer needs cannot be identified unless properly designed questions are put to the customer.

Business success also rests on the quality of staff. Again, the selection, development and performance management of staff cannot be accomplished without key questions being asked in these vital areas (e.g., the job selection interview, training needs identification and the appraisal interview). In summary, properly thought out questions can help businesses gain information, arrive at key facts, clarify issues and assess the judgement of others. These points are explained in detail below:

Reason for question	Example
Gaining Information	"Can you tell me about…?"
Helping a person to relax	"Your record is impressive"
Drawing-out knowledge & experience	"How would you approach…?"
Amplifying/explaining statements	"Explain what you mean by…?"
Keeping the discussion relevant	"Interesting, but lets focus on … ."
Bringing out distinctions	"How would you compare…?"
Re-introducing overlooked points	"I would like to return to…?"
Assessing intelligent judgement	"Let's take the situation where…"
Checking emotional thinking	"How did you feel about that?"

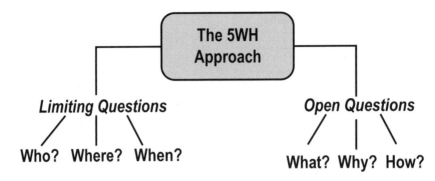

Figure 40: Key question types.

In his poem, *The Elephant's Child*, writer and poet Rudyard Kipling emphasised the importance of 'open'-type questions:

> *I keep six honest serving men*
> *(they taught me all I knew);*
> *Their names are What and Why and When*
> *And How and Where and Who*

Whilst many textbooks emphasise the fact that the '5WH approach' (Kipling's honest men start with five Ws and, of course, the H in How) is an excellent example of the open-question method, on closer examination, however, some aspects of the model are less open than others. Figure 40 confirms this point.

The technique of *linking questions* to the other person's responses can also be very useful. The following example from an interview situation shows how 'linking' can be used to gain insight into a person's attitude—this is also an example of good interview control.

Q. "Why are you applying for another promotion now?"
A. "I have gained a lot of experience, this is the chance to use it and move up … accept more responsibility"
Q. "How would you use this responsibility?"
A. "I would like to be consulted more about what I do and how it's done."
Q. "Doesn't this happen in your present job?"
A. "Not really, my line manager tells me what to do"
Q. "How would you like to be managed then?"
A. "Basically do my own thing … but meet targets, of course."
Q. "What do you think about teamwork?"
A. "It's important for people who aren't that experienced, it gives them support; but people like me should be allowed to get on with things"

The funnel technique

The funnel technique is another example of questions that are planned. Here, however, the questions may not be directly linked. What the questioner is trying to do is to get to a particular point in the discussion; often, this involves a topic that may be sensitive, has some negative aspect to it, or is something the other person may find difficult to speak about. The rationale is to lead-in to the sensitive area by asking non-threatening questions first. Illustration A also highlights the use of the 'open' questions *how, what* and *why*.

Illustration A is an example of the funnel technique being used in a positive manner. Conversely, Illustration B is an example of a more cynical approach, where the motivation of the questioner is to catch the other person out, or engage in 'points-scoring'. This is an approach to avoid. Firstly, because it is not an example of good practice, and secondly, because the person being questioned will soon become aware of what's happening and raise their defences; any potentially valuable information will be lost.

Illustration A – A senior manager has heard about an employee's recent poor appraisal, and knowing him to be a good worker, attempts to informally gain some insight, and perhaps explanation, for the downturn in performance highlighted by his line manager.

Manager:	"*How* are things going?"
Employee:	"Well, they could be better?"
Manager:	"*What* do you mean?"
Employee:	"I didn't get a very good appraisal from Mike?"
Manager:	"*Why* do you think that is?"

Illustration B (Machiavellian) – here, after some preliminary comments, the interviewer springs a key question on the interviewee. By itself, the question about exam failure is not unreasonable, but it is not necessary to place it after the previous positive comments. Putting the question in a different way might not only bring the answer required, but also generate additional information.

Moreover, it may indicate qualities such as self-awareness. For instance, "Are there any areas that you think you could have improved upon?" An important aspect of formal interviews is 'maximising self-disclosure' (getting all the information you can). This will not happen if the interviewee is made uneasy or alarmed by the questions or the interviewing technique used.

"Hope you had a pleasant journey" etc.
"Your appraisals are very positive"
"Your line manager speaks very highly of you"
"Why did you fail your professional exams?"

Question technique—key areas

- Identifying key aspects of the issue and selecting appropriate question types
- Linking questions to responses
- Listening for meaning as well as content
- Using non-verbal behaviour appropriately
- Managing transitions effectively (e.g., "fine, let's go on to…")
- 'Reflecting back' ("So you felt angry about this?")
- Summarising ("So far then…")

As alluded to previously, asking questions is a fundamental human activity. Accorded the importance they deserve in the business setting, intelligent and well designed questions will lead to a better understanding between individuals, the generation of valuable business information and improved individual and company performance.

Listening

To truly understand someone, we must be willing to listen for what they will never be able to say. Listening is sometimes called the forgotten art. In an age of mass communication, there is almost a compulsion to speak. So much so that those who have good listening skills seem exceptionally gifted, rather than just possessing sound communication skills. Listening research shows that many people can only remember 50% of what they have heard shortly afterwards; this can drop significantly again in several months time. Alarmingly, some tests have also revealed that individuals remembered 10% or less of the original message after a few days. There appears to be a number of reasons for this:

Comparison The listener consciously or unconsciously compares what the speaker is saying with their own experiences

Prediction Here, the listener mentally races ahead to try and predict what the speaker is going to say. Sometimes, the listener actually tries to finish the statement for the speaker

Competition The listener tries to trump the comments of the speaker by recounting a similar experience that shows them in a better light

Shutdown This involves the listener mentally shutting off what the speaker is saying in order to prepare their point of view. This can also happen for other reasons, such as lack of interest in the speaker or subject

Selective Perception Sometimes people only hear what they want to hear (what fits in with their own ideas, values or beliefs)

In addition to the above, listener distractions can occur for other reasons such as poor communication on the part of the speaker, those caused by the environment, or poor concentration on the part of the listener. Apart from factors like the environment, training can improve the rest.

Like most of the qualities or skills mentioned in this book, listening has personal as well as business rewards. In the business sense, listening is important for dealing with colleagues, staff, customers and other businesses.

Good listening can help resolve problems when they occur, and even prevent them from arising in the first place (not 'shooting the messenger' is a great personal and business quality). Good listening is also a good motivator, because it sends the signal that the listener cares for what the speaker is saying (and implicitly, them). Good listening helps generate a rich pool of ideas (each of us is not as smart as all of us). Business people need to have as many facts as possible in order to make informed decisions; the lesson is simple, if you don't listen, you won't know all the facts.

In the personal sense, the possession of good listening skills conveys strong messages about who you are as a person. For instance, that you are self aware; that you are approachable; that you have a balanced communication style; that you reach decisions in an informed way; and that you care for others.

Figure 41: The benefits of good listening.

Demonstrating good listening

Active listening is a key component of interpersonal skills. It entails listening for the 'music' as well as the words. This means trying to gain an understanding not only of the words used, but the meaning behind them. It also involves attempts to understand the feelings and emotions that may or may not accompany the words. Sometimes key messages are sent by what remains unsaid. Active listening can be hard work, but as figure 41 confirms, the rewards can be significant. Active listening is demonstrated by:

- Suspending judgement about the person or issue
- Conveying your interest (non-verbal behaviour such as eye contact and nodding is crucial)
- Avoiding interrupting
- Being aware of issues like selective perception (hearing only what you want to hear)
- Concentrating on the main points
- Asking questions where appropriate (plus the techniques used in questioning such as paraphrasing and reflecting-back)

Feedback

Feedback is the sharing of information between two or more people, and is related to matters such as the progress or quality of a conversation, an issue or event; the effect we are having on others; the performance of an individual, group or organisation. Feedback in a business context is vital for key objectives to be reached, for professional development, to identify training needs and to maintain and improve standards. Feedback can be solicited or unsolicited, and unwelcome negative feedback can be very destructive. The real trick is to be able to give negative feedback constructively.

Giving effective feedback involves creating and maintaining a good rapport with those who will receive the feedback. Being specific, using positive non-verbal behaviour and adopting a balanced approach (praise where it is due) are other important factors. People who give feedback effectively are not defensive, and are willing to receive feedback on their own performance. When giving feedback, it is important to:

- Identify what can be changed
- Set SMART objectives (see page 39)
- Avoid exaggeration (e.g., "you're always making mistakes")
- Attack the problem, not the person (if the person is the problem, a counselling approach is best)
- Give it as soon as possible (delay reduces impact)
- Develop an improvement plan
- Always follow up
- Seek feedback on your feedback

Common feedback mistakes

- Waiting until the matter becomes serious
- Using the wrong medium (e.g., email, the telephone)
- Giving negative feedback in front of others
- Lack of specific detail/evidence
- Lack of objectivity

Giving feedback—examples of key statements

Being specific	"The impact on the team was…"
Balanced approach	"Your selling skills are excellent, but perhaps…"
Joint problem solving	"Perhaps if we both worked out a plan to improve…"
Feedback on your Feedback	"Do you think my comments are fair?"

Remember

Positive feedback only will not bring improvement; negative feedback alone can be destructive—adopt a balanced approach.

Summary

- Words alone are not enough to ensure effective communication. Research confirms that a significant degree of personal and work success depends upon our interpersonal skills. Effectiveness in interpersonal skills entails a whole range of learned behaviour, that is goal-directed and appropriate to the situation
- Non-verbal communication is consciously or unconsciously conveying meaning through methods other than words. Such methods consist of one's appearance, facial expressions, eye contact, personal space, gestures, touching and listening

- Communication style is the overall way we behave when we communicate with others. The ability to adjust our communication style in order to effectively relate to people from different backgrounds, culture and level of education is a key communication skill

- Persuasion is a fundamental and legitimate business activity that features in areas such as selling, marketing, advertising and public relations. Ethical persuasion does not involve deceit or pressure, but relies on evidence being presented in a compelling and appropriate manner.

- Although persuasion is an important component of negotiation, negotiation is different in that it is based on the notion that two or more parties have something the other wants. The key to successful negotiation is the willingness to compromise

- Questions underpin a vast range of business activity, from colleague to colleague, informal and formal communication, internal operations and client/customer contact. 'Open' questions such as *what? why?* and *how?* generate more information than 'closed' questions like *who? where?* and *when?*

- The ability to listen effectively is an important business skill, and can help resolve problems when they occur; good listening can even prevent problems occurring in the first place. Effective listening is also a great motivator and can assist in generating a rich pool of ideas

- Feedback is the sharing of information between two or more people. It is related to matters such as the progress and quality of a conversation, issue or event; the effect we can have on others; and the performance of individuals in an organisation. Giving effective feedback involves creating and maintaining a good rapport with listeners, being specific, and using positive non-verbal communication

Tutorial

1. Have someone record a conversation you are having with a friend or business colleague (a camcorder is useful for this). When appraising your performance, try and ascertain the following:

   a. How clear is your voice; how would you describe your tone? how quickly are you speaking; do you have speaking habits such as 'OKs' and 'ahms'; is the volume suitable; what overall image do you convey?

   b. Analyse your non-verbal behaviour by using the following checklist:
      - Eye contact (e.g. confident or weak)
      - Gestures (do they help or hinder?)
      - Posture (do you appear relaxed? confident? tense?)
      - Facial expressions (what do they signal; do they contradict what you are saying?)

   c. Do any of the above vary when you are speaking with particular individuals?

2. One's communication style can vary from situation to situation, what you should be aiming for is an indication of your overall style. Whilst it depends upon the circumstances, a tendency for being frank can signal a direct style (D) or an assertive style (As); being brutally frank indicates an aggressive communication style (Ag). If the answer to f) is yes, then this indicates at least, a direct style (D). There are times when we can get emotional about personal issues, what is important here, is the context and degree. A tendency to often become emotional about personal and work issues could indicate that you have an emotional communication style (E). If you manage to keep your cool under most circumstances, then your overall style is controlled (C). Taking ages to get to the point indicates a passive or indirect style (P/I).

   Trying to assess your communication style is easier for others than for you. However, the following may be useful to consider:

   a. Approximately what percentage do you tend to talk/listen? (what does this tell you?)

   b. Do you tend to interrupt others before they finish? (Ag)

   c. Do you tend to get emotional talking about certain things at work? (E)

   d. Do you 'keep cool' under pressure? (C)

   e. Do you often take a long time to get to the point? (P/I)

   f. Are you always frank whatever the situation or consequences? (D/As/Ag)

3. Select a situation where you need to achieve a goal in the short-term. Achieving this goal requires key persuasion and negotiation skills. With this in mind, devise an action plan that may include the following:
   - A prioritisation of your key needs
   - How you will establish trust
   - What key points you will make (and how)
   - What your communication style should be
   - How you plan to overcome objections
   - What your fall-back position might be (plan B)

4. Review your current approach to questioning, listening and giving/receiving feedback—how could these be improved? (prepare an action plan)

5

Maximise yourself 3—oral presentations

One-minute overview

The credibility of a business organisation consists of many elements (e.g., quality products, good customer care, the integrity of its business practice), not least the credibility of its key people. Whether it's making an in-house project briefing, presenting a business case, or representing the company at a trade or public event, business credibility can be seen to lie in the ability to speak well and hold an audience. Often feared by many competent individuals, oral presentations are less intimidating if viewed in terms of key skills and learned behaviour.

This chapter will help you to recognize the importance of:

- Good planning and preparation
- Considering the audience
- Providing structure
- Using audio-visual aids
- Rehearsing
- Remembering
- Aspects of speech
- Non-verbal communication
- Controlling nerves
- Dealing with questions and interruptions

5.1 Planning and preparing

In addition to enhancing business credibility in general, making presentations develops crucial transferable personal skills such as:

- making a case verbally
- appearing credible to others
- persuading others
- projecting confidence
- using non-verbal behaviour positively
- anticipating and overcoming negative responses
- using different media (e.g. diagrams/charts)
- dealing with questions

Consequently, the skills associated with presentations enable one to capitalise on existing knowledge and expertise; optimise your input in briefings, meetings, marketing presentations and other 'public performances'; improve personal effectiveness at work and in a variety of social settings.

Effective presentations consist of a number of important aspects:

- **Clarification of aims and objectives**
- **Effective research**
- **Considering the audience**
- **Sound planning and preparation**
- **Identification of the skills required**
- **A clear structure**
- **Effective time management**
- **Anticipating potential problems**

There is a strong link between effective planning and successful presentations. Whilst good planning in itself cannot guarantee success, it does increase the likelihood of the presentation being effective. Planning and preparation involves careful thought about the key presentation issues mentioned previously:

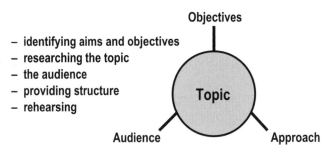

- identifying aims and objectives
- researching the topic
- the audience
- providing structure
- rehearsing

Aims and objectives

Making a presentation is usually more than just giving a talk; whether intended or not, it invariably results in some sort of change. Simply giving information about a topic, for example, can result in knowledge being improved or awareness being raised. Consequently, the main considerations are: what change is intended, what are the desired outcomes? Presentation aims can range from wanting to inform and persuade to increasing confidence, relieving anxiety or changing attitudes.

Aims and objectives—key questions

- What is the desired outcome?
- How can it be best achieved?
- How can I translate objectives into learning points?
- What are the main points I need to make?
- Is there an overall strategy? (e.g., inform, persuade, motivate)
- How can I check that my aims and objectives have been reached? (e.g., questions)

Researching the topic

Even if you are familiar with the topic, it is still important to gather plenty of information and that the information is from more than one source. This, of course, applies to the planning stage only; *a presentation crowded with too much information will sink under its own weight.* Many presenters prefer to have a lot of information to begin with, and then reduce this to key issues and points. Whatever your knowledge base, researching information helps refresh the mind about what is relevant, identify the main points and order their sequence for logical delivery. Although it depends upon the preparation time available, there are many and varied sources of information: from personal notes to company, library and media sources. Figure 42 illustrates some of these.

Figure 42:

Whatever information is generated, it must be remembered that it will be best received if it is supported by evidence and appropriately linked to personal experience (avoid the repetition of dry facts where possible).

Research checklist ✓

- Research widely
- Note the source
- Identify a use for each item (e.g., handout, visual aid etc.)
- Reduce information to key points
- Support key points with evidence

Considering the audience

In a manner of speaking, the audience *is* the presentation; whatever one wishes to convey, no matter how important it is deemed to be, all will be to little avail if the composition, needs and expectations of the audience are not given due consideration. Therefore, the information given during a presentation should be based as much as possible on the information gained about the audience (e.g., subject knowledge, level of education).

Researching the audience is vital for ensuring that:

- aims and objectives are clarified
- the appropriate content is selected
- the presentation is pitched at the correct level
- boredom or offence is avoided
- adequate numbers are catered for

Audience research

Key Aspects	*Key Questions*
Background Details	– What is the age range?
	– What is their general level of education/training?
	– What kind of approach should be used? (e.g., clear examples)
	– What degree of formality would be appropriate?

Indicative Content	– How much do they already know about the topic?
	– How much do they need to know?
	– How much additional knowledge is required?
	– Are there any additional defined or potential needs?
Potential Reaction	– Have they been forced to attend?
	– How objective are they?
	– What is their likely attention span?
	– How much information could they handle?

Other important aspects of audience research are the size of the audience and the nature of the venue. Size has implications in terms of equipment, handouts etc., but it can also influence your presentation style and general approach. Where the venue is concerned, it is advisable to:

– check for any potential noise or disruptions
– arrange the seating so that the audience is concentrated
– check heating, ventilation etc.
– sit where the audience sits, is the presenter's position suitable?
– check for black-out curtains if visual aids are to be used
– if a sound system is to be used, check that it is working effectively

Audience checklist ✓

Profile the audience – How might they differ in their needs and expectations?
Clarify objectives – By the end of the presentation, the audience should…
Plan and organise – Good planning and organisation makes the presenter appear confident, credible and professional
Identify the Strategy – Informing? persuading? changing attitudes? etc.
Appreciate them – Talk *to* them, not at them
Guide them – Use signposts, e.g., "first of all I will…, then…, and finally…"
Be natural – Be as natural as you can in the circumstances and avoid pretence
Be enthusiastic – Enthusiasm, like humour, is infectious (but use humour carefully)

Providing structure

Once sufficient information has been generated by research, the next stage is to provide some sort of structure. Structure is important in two main respects: to enable the presenter to impart the information in a logical manner, and to help the audience follow the material presented. It is important to ensure that:

– the material is concise, clear and relevant
– there is a logical sequence
– interim summaries are provided (e.g. "so far then…")
– where appropriate, visual aids are used

Structure can be viewed in the general sense of the *three-stage approach* (introduction, development and conclusion), and in the particular sense of a 'script' containing the sequence of the main points and supporting details.

Introduction

Along with the closing remarks, the opening statements tend to be the more memorable of any presentation and should be designed to capture the audience's attention. Unless you know the audience well, do not use jokes or startling comments; the best approach is to provide a clear outline of what the presentation is about, and state any limitations or restrictions. For example, if you prefer to leave questions to the end, then this limitation should be stated at the outset.

Development

Whilst the style of the presenter can help concentration, attention tends to drops as the presentation continues. It is vital therefore to develop the main points clearly and logically; provide linking words and phrases between points; use visual evidence where appropriate; and provide interim summaries. The way some comments are structured, along with the repetition of key words and phrases, are valuable techniques for holding an audience during the development stage.

Conclusion

The end of a presentation provides an opportunity to refocus the audience on the key points. The audience has been listening to the presenter for some time; therefore, the conclusion must be as short and powerful as possible. Although handouts may be provided emphasising the main points, the aim of a good conclusion is to give the audience an impressive but simple mental package that they can take away with them and ponder over.

The following is an example of a simple, but logical sequence:

Introduction	– Opening pleasantries
	– Statement of objectives
	– Outline of presentation
	– Mention of any limitations
Development	– Development of key points
	– Evidence for position adopted (if relevant)
	– Coverage of opposing views (if necessary)
	– Interim summaries (e.g., "I would now like to examine…")
Conclusion	– Final summary of main points
	– Restate/outline position
	– Weigh-up evidence
	– Conclude (thank them and invite questions)

Creating the 'Script'

A detailed structure can be arrived at either by writing the planned comments out in full and then reducing them into key points; or, conversely, starting off with the selected key points and then adding the detail. Whichever method is preferred, both have the benefit of improving content knowledge (the more you read, the more you remember). However, the term script is an unfortunate one since some people take it to mean that it should merely be read; and this, regrettably, is what some presenters do. As can be seen in the delivery section, reading a script is *not* making a presentation.

5.2 Audio visual aids

Audio-visual aids not only enhance presentations, but in some cases, are vitally necessary to communicate complex information (e.g., pie charts to explain statistics). Audio visual aids serve a number of useful functions, they:

- Provide focal points for the presentation
- Reinforce key issues
- Clarify complex matters
- Help the audience to remember
- Make the presenter look professional
- Take the pressure off the presenter

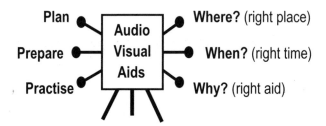

Although audio visual aids help illustrate and reinforce the presenter's comments, a careful balance must be maintained between the aids and the comments. If visual aids are not planned and used selectively, the focus shifts from the presenter to the aid in an unbalanced way. The aid, then, becomes the presentation. Visual aids also play an important role as a timing device. They introduce pauses into a presentation, giving the audience a rest from the presenter's voice and allowing them to reflect on the points made. A range of audio-visual aids are available, and the most common are:

Flipchart	Whiteboard
Overhead projector	Computer-linked projector (e.g., PowerPoint)
Tape/slide projector	Video tapes and films
Tape recorders	Models/samples

Microsoft powerpoint

Whilst the use of the traditional overhead projector (OHP) has diminished significantly in recent years, the rise of the Microsoft PowerPoint presentation package has been somewhat spectacular. Indeed, for most business professionals, it has become *the* tool for oral presentations. Reasons for this include its ease of use, its professional impact and its flexibility.

Although there are many books on the market explaining how PowerPoint works, the package itself is quite simple to use. This is because it has many help features, wizards and templates; basically, if you can Illustration A word process, you can use PowerPoint. Illustration A shows how the user just has to click the chosen format in order to start the presentation. Choices include a range of pre-prepared layouts, or a blank template where the user can add their own design.

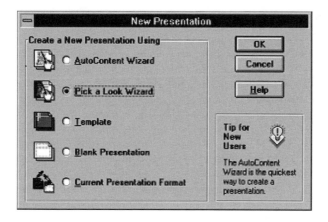

Illustration A:

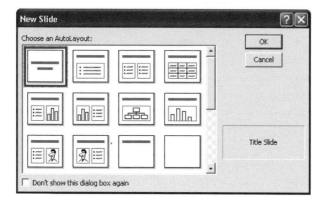

Illustration B:

Illustration A also indicates the range of auto-layouts available, these include:

The AutoContent Wizard – this creates specific formats for occasions such as training or sales

The Pick a Look Wizard – slides are already created with a consistent appearance

Template – here, the slide show can be built from templates where the colour scheme, font etc. are pre-selected

AutoLayouts (illustration B) allow the user to select the structure for a single slide. For instance, you may wish to have a list of bullet points and a diagram or graphic on the same slide; AutoLayout will allow you to do this.

Illustration C shows the PowerPoint easy-to-use interface. As with most Microsoft features, all the user has to do is move the cursor over the button, and its function will be explained. Users familiar with Microsoft Word will find the typical PowerPoint interface quite similar, with some added features. For example, 'insert' allows graphics, photos, video clips and diagrams etc. to Illustration C be imported into the selected slide(s).

Selecting 'view' (slide sorter) allows the user to gain an overview of the various slides and rearrange their sequence. When adding text, clicking the facility '*slide show*',

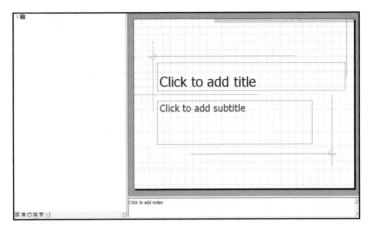

Illustration C:

and then '*custom animation*', allows the user to determine how the text will appear (e.g., appear immediately, slowly, fade out etc.). Most importantly, PowerPoint has a facility for adding speaker notes.

Although a computer and projector are needed to optimise the impact of PowerPoint (a television can also be used), it is still very flexible. For instance: files can be held in a simple memory stick or sent as attachments; files can be converted to PDF (portable document format) to share with others; file security can be added (PowerPoint 2007 enables digital signatures); the relatively new XM format allows file size to be significantly reduced; professional handouts can be produced with several slides on each page; presentations can be saved as web pages. As with all computer packages, the best way to become proficient with PowerPoint is to use it.

Optimising presentation impact

No matter how sophisticated the presentation tool, *how* the tool is used is vital for optimising impact. For example, the following tend to switch audiences off:

- Simply reading what's on the slide/transparency/flipchart (no 'added value')
- Printing long sentences instead of bullet-points
- Using text that is too small
- Using inappropriate colours for the text or background
- Putting too much information on one slide/transparency/flipchart
- Lack of consistency in slide design
- Using overly complex information or diagrams
- Using gimmicks that distract (e.g., flying text or noise effects in PowerPoint)
- Too many PowerPoint slides ('death by PowerPoint')

Keeping audiences interested involves good preparation, good timing and an effective grasp of the topic. The following are tips for optimising presentation impact:

- Plan the sequence of the overall message, the material used should reflect this (e.g., PowerPoint slides)
- Keep things simple (e.g., one slide, one set of ideas)

- Stick to one type of font (e.g., using Arial prevents blurring when projected)
- The main font should be about 30 pt
- Use a larger font for titles
- Have a good contrast between font and coloured background
- Use bold and colour to provide emphasis
- Avoid too much detail or rows of statistics
- For important presentations, copy PowerPoint slides to colour transparencies*

*PowerPoint has a very powerful impact, but technical problems can happen. Having a copy of your presentation in transparency format means that, with a traditional OHP, you can still get your message across and appear just as professional. Remember, the simplest presentations are often the most effective.

It is important to remember the different ways in which information can be presented

- contrasts can greatly enhance understanding of the overall situation
- devices such as bar charts and pie charts help the audience to make comparisons and understand complicated information (e.g., statistics)
- diagrams, flow charts and illustrations are particularly useful for aiding under-standing of a sequence of events

Writing during a presentation—checklist ✓

- Keep spare chalk and pens
- Position the body carefully
- Plan the size of your writing (view it from the back of the room)
- Write first of all, then comment (doing both together may be impressive, but it can confuse the audience)
- Outline any diagrams in pencil first (flip chart)

5.3 Rehearsing

Even confident presenters appreciate the importance of rehearsing; particularly when adding new aspects to existing material, or if the presentation has significant ramifications. No matter how effective planning and other aspects of preparation are then, the potential impact of the presentation cannot be accurately assessed without a rehearsal. Rehearsing is especially useful for:

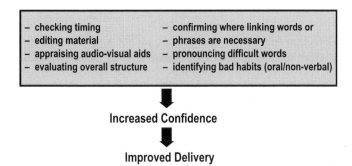

- checking timing
- editing material
- appraising audio-visual aids
- evaluating overall structure

- confirming where linking words or phrases are necessary
- pronouncing difficult words
- identifying bad habits (oral/non-verbal)

Increased Confidence

Improved Delivery

Rehearsal—checklist ✓

- Familiar with equipment?
- Material effectively edited?
- Visual aids satisfactory?
- Appropriate memory aids?
- Particular aspects of time noted?
- Difficult words/phrases/material identified?
- Negative verbal/non-verbal habits noted?

5.4 Delivery

Poor presenting behaviour can be viewed in terms of certain types. Examples in this respect are:

The Racer   Going to get to end no matter what

The Rambler   Moves from one point to another with no clear structure

The Rambo   Over-enthusiastic; attacks the script and almost does the same to the audience (uncontrolled non-verbal behaviour)

The Reader   Glued to their notes, which results in a dry, boring delivery

The Rector   Preaches at the audience

The Rookie   Inexperienced and shows it; appears a nervous wreck

The Rumbler   Rumbles along in a monotone, almost inaudible voice

Effective delivery can be seen to be composed of key components

Remembering	e.g. Impressing the audience with a clear command of the facts (with minimal aids)
Communication style	e.g. Command of language, exuding trust, credibility, and inspiring confidence
Personality traits	e.g. Conveying enthusiasm, warmth and energy; the ability to develop a good relationship with the audience
Non-verbal behaviour	e.g. Deliberate, positive use of non-verbal behaviour to support speech and hold the audience
Aspects of voice	e.g. Using volume and tone to cue, emphasise and create atmosphere
Timing	e.g. Using audio visual aids, pauses and silence to maximise effect

> Handouts are best distributed at the end of the presentation. Giving them out during the presentation can negatively affect your delivery and audience concentration

> **Remember**
> Closely associated with nervousness, failure to remember is probably one of the most feared aspects of making presentations. Relying solely on memory (helped

by minimal aids) is a method favoured by some presenters, but as the section on preparation indicates, it has drawbacks:

- it requires significant concentration and expertise
- important points can be missed
- the structure of the presentation can be unclear
- the potential for disaster is greatly increased

What many presenters feel uncomfortable with is the memorising of the main presentation stages and key points. This memory base can be supplemented by the variety of audio-visual aids such as flipcharts and cue cards; such aids can be subtly applied after some experience. However, if you are inexperienced, care needs to be taken with aids such as cue cards. The most effective way of using cue cards is to use them in a forthright manner; thus creating the impression that they *are* a natural part of the presentation. As some presenters have found to their cost, using cue cards involves a number of sensible precautions:

- write only on one side
- use highlighting and spacing to aid reading
- punch a hole in the corner of each card and secure with string or treasury tags
- use the key point approach
- number each card

Aspects of speech

Different areas relating to delivery have already been considered, and important though they are, the main method of communication where presentations are concerned is the human voice. Speaking effectively means following a number of separate but related strategies.

You have to:

Articulate　Speaking as clearly as you can under the circumstances; uncontrolled nerves can cause you to be inarticulate

Pronounce **Properly**　No matter how good our command of English is, various words can cause problems with respect to pronunciation. Where this is likely to be the case, try to find other words to replace them (use a thesaurus) or break the word down and rehearse

Vary Pitch and Tone　Nothing is more boring than listening to a person speaking in a monotonous voice. Try to make your voice more interesting

Enunciate　Add emphasis to certain words and phrases; for example:

"**I** think this is important"

"I **think** this is important"

"I think **this** is important"

Repeat　As with written work, repetition must be used selectively and sparingly. Repetition is particularly useful where inspiration is required:

"*We* have the ability to succeed, *we* have the resolve to succeed, *we* will succeed" (use of emphasis and personalisation as well as repetition, i.e., "we").

Project　Wherever they sit, everyone must be able to hear you; project your voice. Voice volume must be appropriate for the room and the size of the audience;

it must also not be too forceful or over-bearing. Changes in volume can also be used for emphasis, providing links and signalling transitions

Pause   Timed correctly, it can create an air of expectancy and focus attention. It is important to consider using pauses:

– at the start of the presentation (especially if full attention is not given)
– before making a key point (the build-up approach)
– after giving a complex piece of information (allows the audience 'brain time')
– towards the end of the presentation (facilitates consideration of the key issues)

Improving aspects of speech such as articulation entails exercises like:

– shaping the words more than you might do normally (use the lips more)
– increasing the emphasis on consonants
– reducing speaking speed
– using short pauses, especially between difficult words or phrases

Other exercises, such as control of breathing, use of the lips, throat etc., are important supporting strategies in achieving maximum vocal effect.

Aspects of speech—focus points

- Use words/phrases/sentences that are simple and clear
- Informing is more important than impressing (use an economy of words)
- Deliver in a style that is appropriate to the audience
- If technical terms have to be used, explain them briefly (but do not patronise)
- Avoid jargon, slang and 'in-words'
- Avoid pet words and phrases (e.g., "obviously", "quite apparent")
- Use techniques such as emphasis and pauses (but carefully consider where)
- Vary pitch and tone
- Speak loud enough to be heard (but volume must be appropriate to room and audience size)

5.5 Non-verbal communication (NVC)

Whilst *what* the presenter says is important, *how* the information is delivered is crucial in terms of supporting the presenter's overall 'message'. Some aspects of *how* have already been described, but the significance of NVC is not to be underestimated. Although our voice is important, we communicate with our whole body.

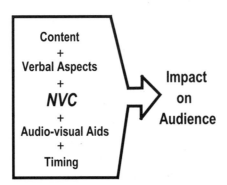

NVC includes all the 'body language' that people purposely or unconsciously convey. Despite the fact that the term non-verbal *behaviour* (NVB) is sometimes used to denote body language that the individual is unaware of, NVC is the generally accepted comprehensive description of this important form of human communicating behaviour.

When we meet others (especially for the first time), whether we are conscious of the fact or not, we are communicating, receiving and interpreting a whole range of non-verbal signals such as facial expressions (particularly eye contact), gestures, and various other aspects of personal appearance. It is worth remembering that, as well as supporting what the presenter says, NVC can also undermine or even contradict what is stated verbally. This is the uncontrolled aspect of NVC, sometimes referred to as 'leakage' (in spite of the person's attempts at control, contradictory signals leak out).

Facial expressions

There appears to be almost universal understanding of what most facial expressions mean (e.g., happiness, sadness, fear, surprise etc.). Experienced presenters are very much aware that facial movements involving smiles, nods and eye contact reveal attitude. For example, smiles that are appropriately given and well-timed can demonstrate that the presenter is human and has a sense of humour; they are vital for 'unfreezing' the audience and building a good relationship.

Eye Contact—focus points

Eye contact is vital for:

- Confirming the presenter's confidence
- Building a bond with the audience
- Holding the audience's attention
- Reinforcing key points
- Supporting the credibility of the message

Try to avoid:

- concentrating on individuals sitting at the front
- ignoring members of the audience at the back or sides of the room
- letting eye contact turn into a gaze

Posture   As with many aspects of non-verbal behaviour, it is difficult to control our natural posture; particularly when we are over-anxious or under pressure. Try to adopt a position that is as natural as possible in the circumstances, but manages to avoid those elements of posture that tend to create an unfavourable impression

It is important, therefore, that you:

- squarely and confidently face the audience (especially at the beginning)
- avoid slouched positions where possible (even if trying to communicate informality)
- do not pace up and down; this tends to unsettle the audience (and seriously affects posture)
- avoid gripping lecterns etc. (this tends to transmit a wooden appearance)
- breathe deeply (but subtly), this relaxes the body and helps control posture

Gestures

Despite the fact that gestures can be made with most parts of the body, the hands tend to be the most expressive (and distracting). Pointing to visuals and supporting speech are examples of positive gestures that help build the relationship with the audience. Conversely, too many gestures can convey an almost comical impression, which undermines both the message and the presenter. Audiences are quite capable of decoding involuntary as well as intended NVC, and gestures tend to be less subtle than some other forms of NVC. Consequently, a careful balance must be struck between over-use of gestures and the adoption of an almost lifeless appearance.

NVC—focus points

- Clothes send messages about the presenter—dress appropriately
- Adopt a confident posture (do not slouch or appear wooden)
- Avoid pacing up and down
- Smiles are invaluable for developing rapport (but they must appear natural)
- Controlled nodding can be used to regulate feedback from the audience
- Maintain regular eye contact with the audience
- Keep gestures to a minimum

5.6 Nerves

It is possible to be well prepared and confident, yet still nervous; indeed, most presenters feel some degree of nervousness before a presentation. This is not a bad thing, since it helps concentrate the mind and prevents the presenter from becoming over-confident. Nerves, then, keep the presenter alert and tuned-in to the audience. Nerves tend to be more of a problem before the presentation than during it, and this is one reason why they usually diminish as the presentation continues; for some, however, nerves remain a serious matter.

Potential Problem	Recommended Strategy
Poor audience reaction	– Keep thinking: "I've prepared well and rehearsed" – practise positive NVC to develop rapport – commit the opening lines to memory – speak *to* the audience
Memory loss	– Consider the range of memory aids – Use the memory aid you prefer – Plan any visuals so as to provide 'thinking time' – Keep back-up notes close at hand
Getting the sequence wrong	– Avoid complicated sequences if possible – Use a visual for prioritised lists (complex ones on handouts) – Do not panic (only you know the exact sequence) – Use a comment like, "at this point, I am not referring to these in any particular order"
Speech problems	– Always have a glass of water at hand (but sip slowly) – Slow down – Breathe deeply – Think of the key words or concept

Equipment malfunctions	– Again, do not panic, make light of the problem
	– Plan for problems: keep spares if possible (e.g., bulbs for OHP, copies of PowerPoint slides on transparencies, etc.)
	– Use an additional method for key facts (e.g., handouts)
	– View the problem as an opportunity to impress, e.g., "these things sometimes happen, I will now use the flipchart/handout to reinforce the key points contained in the video I was going to show"

Nerves—focus points

- Feeling nervous is natural (and to a certain extent, necessary)
- Use personal relaxation strategies before presentations (e.g., listening to music)
- Identify personal symptoms of nervousness (develop strategies to overcome them)
- Reduce any feelings of nervousness during the presentation by breathing deeply and concentrating on the task in hand
- Feel confident and you will appear confident

5.7 Dealing with questions

Because by their nature questions are unpredictable, they are difficult to prepare for. However, as with all aspects of a presentation, the key to success is effective planning. One of the fundamental planning issues is whether to allow questions during the presentation, or at the end. Another important planning element is the amount of time allocated to questions. Whilst it is not possible to anticipate questions in an exact way, it may be possible to anticipate, in a broad sense, the type and range of questions the audience might ask. Again, a vital factor here is the presenter's topic knowledge. It is also useful for the presenter to *ask themselves questions*. For example:

- what are the key issues?
- are there any problem issues?
- what issues have had to be left out? (time constraint)
- what questions would I find the most difficult to answer? (more 'home work' required)
- what questions would I ask, if I were in the audience?

Dealing with questions—key points

Listen Carefully	In addition to hearing the actual words, perceptive listening may be required to identify any particular views or assumptions that may lie behind a particular question **Strategy:** practise active listening (*listen for meaning* as well as the actual words used)
Equal Opportunity	Do not allow one member of the audience to 'hog' question time. Not only is this frustrating for other members, but the guilty party is using your time to make a mini presentation of their own

	Strategy: Use the time factor to move on, e.g., "I'm sorry but you have been given a fair amount of time"
Keep Control	In addition to the possibility of some questioners being hostile to the presenter, they may also be hostile to each other; using the presentation to score points
	Strategy:
	a. Use the time factor mentioned above
	b. Invite questions from other members
	c. Threaten to terminate question time (actually, do this as a last resort)
Difficult Questions	If you do not know the answer to a question, say so. If you feel you can give a reasonable answer, but need thinking time, then play for time. If the question entails a 'no win' situation, then seek to avoid answering it (politicians do it all the time)
	Strategy:
	a. *Be honest* if you do not know the answer
	b. If you can attempt an answer, you may wish to play for time by asking the questioner to explain what they mean
	c. If you wish to gauge the strength of feeling about an issue, ask how many others feel the same
	d. If you do not wish to answer a question directly, throw it to the audience and then summarise
	e. If you are forced to answer, the best course is to empathise and give a neutral reply, e.g., "Whilst I understand the views behind the question are valid, perhaps the best course of action is…"

Coping with interruptions

Despite the ground rules set by the presenter, questions or comments may not come at the requested time. In short, the presenter must have some sort of strategy to deal with interruptions. Indeed, how this is accomplished can seriously affect the credibility of the presenter; it also often indicates their self-confidence and experience. Consequently, although most audiences resent interruptions and hostile questions (and are therefore on the presenter's side), presenters must have a series of alternative responses to combat such situations. Above all, the presenter *must not lose their 'cool'* (rather than a member of the audience defeating the presenter, the presenter has defeated themselves).

Examples regarding alternative responses are:

– the use of humour (but do not patronise)
– make a positive response, e.g., "I'm glad you have asked this question because it gives me the opportunity to…"
– 'kill them with kindness', i.e., highlight their lack of grace by demonstrating your tolerance, patience and good manners
– outflank them, e.g., "If you *all* wish me to deal with this question now, I will, but perhaps you might wish me to continue as agreed, and outline the key

points first?" (use of non-verbal communication aspects such as eye contact are crucial here)

Question time—focus points

- Seek feedback if necessary
- Decide when questions are to be asked (make this clear to the audience)
- Develop a range of strategies to deal with potential problems
- Keep control of the audience
- Handle interruptions courteously and professionally (but firmly)
- Do not waffle (be honest if you do not know the answer)

Summary

- Presentations are crucial for establishing business credibility
- Presentations develop other transferable skills
- Presentations can involve objectives such as behavioural change
- Planning and preparation are vital for success
- The audience need 'signposts' and an easy-to-follow structure
- Audio-visual aids can reinforce key points and help take the pressure off the presenter
- Rehearsing pays dividends such as increased confidence and improved performance
- Effective delivery entails a good grasp of content, using the voice to maximum effect and adopting positive aspects of non-verbal communication
- Memory can be improved by using a range of techniques such as flipcharts, the overhead projector and cue cards
- Speaking effectively means following a number of separate, but related strategies. For example, varying pitch and tone, and adding emphasis to certain words or phrases
- A key element in how the information is delivered and perceived is non-verbal communication; aspects such as eye contact are critical in this respect
- Nervousness can be alleviated through rehearsal and deep-breathing exercises
- Dealing with questions can be made less stressful by using strategies like throwing the question back at the questioner or the audience, and then summarising

Tutorial

1. Determine the overall strategy of your next presentation (e.g., to impartially inform, persuade, enthuse etc.) and then identify what impact this has on aspects such as speech, opening comments, conclusions etc.
2. The voice is a key factor in presentation success, make it sound more interesting by using a tape recorder to practise changes in pitch, tone, speed etc.
3. Assess the effectiveness of your delivery by using a video camera or the help of friends. An appraisal checklist along the following lines might be useful:

		Comments
Introduction	e.g. statement of objectives	....
Voice	e.g. clarity, speed, tone	....
Content	e.g. relevant, well-organised	....
Structure	e.g. clear logical order	....
Transitions	e.g. linking words/phrases	....
Time	e.g. too long? too short?	....
Non-verbal behaviour	e.g. eye contact	....
Audio-visual aids	e.g. clarity, number	....
Memory aids	e.g. effectively used?	....
Summary	e.g. key points re-emphasised	....

Maximising the business 1

One-minute overview

A business is the sum total, not just of its products, services, or collective expertise, but also of its core values, sense of direction and its customer orientation. In practical terms, an organisation's core values and sense of direction are enshrined in its mission statement. This outlines why it exists, where it wants to go, and key goals and objectives. However critical such factors are, one additional element has always been necessary for business success—trust. Research confirms that trust is a prime means of judging business organisations, is an important source of competitive advantage, and is crucial for building and reinforcing customer loyalty. Accordingly, if businesses are to flourish, they will have to maximise the key factors of vision, trust and customer orientation. Once again, communication plays a pivotal role in this whole process.

This chapter will enable you to:

- Realise the importance of the envisioning process
- Identify the key skills and methods associated with the envisioning process
- Appreciate the necessity of building and maintaining trust
- Be aware of the different forms that trust can take
- Develop the skills of trust-building behaviour
- Recognise how trust can be undermined
- Appreciate the value of customer orientation
- Understand what customers want
- Realise what business organisations need to do to enhance customer orientation
- Understand the importance of communication in the above processes

6.1 Creating the vision

One of the most important concepts an organisation can communicate is its vision. A vision statement projects the image of where the business will be some time in the future (e.g., five or ten years). It can reflect the desired market position (e.g., 'the number one in…'), the customer focus to be adopted and the relevant business activities to be pursued. Vision statements can also reflect core values such as integrity, service, quality, social responsibility, excellence and innovation. The genuine adoption and promotion of core values is central to the vision. Consequently, for the vision to be successful, core values need to inform not just aspects like goals, decisions, priorities and behaviour, but the very culture of the organisation.

Having a clear vision of the future is just as important for small to medium enterprises (SMEs), and even the sole entrepreneur, as it is for large organisations. Business visions

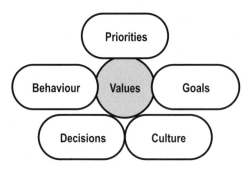

Figure 43: Values need to inform key activities.

differ from business dreams in that they are based on reality, and have concrete aims and objectives. A vision is a definition of an ideal state, and it helps set the direction of the business. Companies identify the need for a vision for a variety of reasons: the business wishes to expand, the business has grown significantly, a new strategic direction is required, or the business is in a turnaround situation.

Vision statements are indispensable for:

- Creating a strategic vision of what the organisation will look like in the future
- Mapping-out the long-term direction of the organisation
- Articulating the organisation's passion for the product or service
- Providing a renewed sense of purpose
- Indicating and mobilising the resources required to achieve the vision
- Indicating the degree of change required
- Inspiring internal and external stakeholders into action
- Identifying key goals and objectives
- Providing focus for decision-making

Mini Glossary	
Mission	Defines why an organisation exists
Vision	Summarises the ideal state of an organisation (where they want to be)
Strategic Plan	How the organisation can achieve the vision
Goals	Transforms the vision into achievable targets
Objectives	Reduces goals into tasks that are measurable and time-related (see page 39)

Those who are responsible for the envisioning process (the 'vision leader') can be seen to go through three distinct stages: developing the vision, communicating the vision and making the organisational changes necessary for the vision to be realised (e.g., developing strategy, setting goals and breaking down organisational barriers). Realising the vision often means radical change, and this creates other key activities for the vision leader like identifying and empowering 'change agents', and conducting organisational analysis (re-read pages 37 & 38 for details of SWOT analysis).

The Mission statement

An organisation's mission statement is an important part of its strategic plan, and its aim is to define the specific purpose of a business by capturing its goals and philosophy in a few sentences. A mission statement provides a template for defining, initiating and evaluating the organisation's core activities.

Mission statements also reflect the core competencies and passion behind the business; they can identify who the customer is and define standards of performance. They should be flexible enough to allow for new products and services, yet, at the same time, provide focus for what drives the business. For example, Ben and Jerry's Ice Cream mission statement identifies that they not only make the ice cream, but distribute and sell it as well. In addition, it stresses that it uses natural ingredients and is a responsible business with a commitment to the environment—these are the key drivers.

'To make, distribute and sell the finest quality all natural ice cream and euphoric concoctions with a continued commitment to incorporating wholesome, natural ingredients and promoting business practices that respect the Earth and the environment'

One way of viewing the difference between vision and mission is to see the vision as consisting of the 'what', and the mission consisting of the 'how'. The mission statement of the McKinsey Consulting Group clearly identifies what it does, and the benefits of what it does: *'To help our clients make positive, lasting and substantial improvements in their performance and build a great firm that is able to attract, develop, excite and retain exceptional people'*. Sometimes, mission statements include visionary aspects as well; if this is the case, then there is no need for a separate vision statement. Effective mission statements need to answer key questions such as:

— what is the purpose of the business?
— who does the business serve; who are the customers?
— what needs does the business fulfil?
— how are those needs fulfilled?
— what values drive the business?

Key stages of the vision process

1 *Creating the vision focus team*

Creating an effective vision statement requires the generation of quality information and time investment. This entails bringing together all the key stakeholders within the business enterprise. In order to optimise buy-in to the vision, it is important that representatives from all areas of the business are included. Consideration should also be given to the interests of external stakeholders such as customers/clients and suppliers. External stakeholders provide focus for the needs to be met; consideration of internal stakeholders helps to identify the key change agents necessary for the vision to be realised. Important roles of the vision focus team include:

Refining – distilling disparate views and opinions
Defining – focusing on key aspects of the vision
Assigning – delegating the key tasks for realising the vision concept

If the business form is one of sole entrepreneur or a small enterprise, it is important to have others give their opinion on the final vision statement. This is to prevent 'tunnel vision', and the fact that the vision may not consider serious obstacles. However, there are many examples of sole entrepreneurs or small enterprises where the visionaries just 'went with the dream' (e.g., Ben and Jerry's Ice Cream, Trevor Bayliss' wind-up radio and James Dyson's revolutionary vacuum cleaner). In other words, there are occasions when the visionary's passion and self belief is such that they appear to overcome significant barriers by sheer will alone.

2 *Identifying methods and skills*

It is vital that the focus team include people who have a mixture of skills and talents. Creative thinking and problem solving are just as important as logical approaches. This is because logical problem solving is often associated with problems that are 'closed' (answers are the logical outcome of stated or known facts). Creative thinking tends to be more appropriate when the issue or problem is 'open' (the relevant facts may be unknown, imprecise or in dispute). Creative thinking requires the desire to question the 'obvious', intuition and imagination—key aspects of envisioning. One example of creative thinking is visualising the situation where the vision is realised, and then working backwards. This can help identify key challenges and the formulation of plans to meet and overcome these.

Methods like 'flip-charting', mind-maps (where thoughts are represented as patterns) and personal and group brainstorming are crucial processes. Brainstorming has certain rules, for example: all ideas are to be considered (no matter how 'way-out' they may be); think laterally (e.g., look for what is different or unusual); and change emphasis from one part of the issue to another (e.g., what is *not* a problem).

Seeking solutions involves critical skills such as listening, reflecting and decision-making. In addition, the following skills are invaluable:

Perception   identifying different facets of a problem or issue and perceiving different alternatives or solutions

Synthesis   whilst analysis involves breaking things down in order to examine them closely, synthesis entails reconstructing the various elements of an issue or problem, and considering how one or more elements affect others

Evaluating & deciding   considering the relative merits of information, alternatives and potential solutions; and reaching the best decision in the circumstances

Here, again, the '5WH' method can also prove very useful:

Why   do we need the vision?

What   message(s) do we want the vision to convey?

When   are we going to launch the vision? (timing is crucial; consider aspects like market conditions and the performance of the business)

Where   are we going to launch the vision?

Who   are the key 'vision agents' (those who will help reinforce the vision messages) and audiences?

How   do we communicate and reinforce the vision? (e.g., methods; internal and external aspects)

3 *Writing the vision statement*

Vision statements are about capturing dreams, and, therefore, they need to be inspirational, motivational and reflect your beliefs and values. In recent years, many vision statements appear to be just a collection of clichés or platitudes (or both). So much so that it is difficult to separate one organisation from another. Consequently, the language of vision statements is extremely important and needs to be positive, contain descriptors that indicate what the organisation wants to achieve, signal intent about achieving it and generate confidence in the organisation. Amazon's vision statement may be relatively short, but its intent is quite clear: *'Our vision is to be earth's most customer centric; to build a place where people can come to find and discover anything they might want to buy online'.*

Whether the final vision statement takes the form of a short paragraph, a few bullet points, or a single sentence, it must be clear, focused and easily understood. The 'Cs of communication' are very useful here: *clear, concise, comprehensive* (covering the key mission points), *comprehensible* (simple language). Vision statement language tends to contain 'action words'; for example, 'to be the *number one…*'; 'to achieve *maximum growth*'; '…and in doing so, to *serve* the community'. Action words also serve to express key visionary goals, and these tend to fall into certain categories.

Examples in this respect are:

Target-setting   e.g. 'To be number one service provider in the catering industry'
Role-modelling   e.g. 'To be the Rolls Royce of electrical component providers'
Radical Change   e.g. 'To bring innovative solutions to the marketplace'

Writing the vision statement—Checklist ✓

- Does it accurately convey what the organisation wants to achieve?
- Does it set the organisation apart from others in the same field?
- Does the statement clearly reflect the organisation's values?
- Does it signal positive change?
- Does it communicate customer/client focus?
- Will it enthuse and empower employees and focus their energies?
- Will it inspire and motivate other key stakeholders?
- Is the language simple?
- Is it free of clichés and platitudes?

4 Communicating the vision statement

> *"Without question, communicating the vision and the atmosphere around the vision has been, and is continuing to be, by far the toughest job we face"*
>
> Jack Welch
> (whilst chairman of General Electric)

There is a major difference between an organisation with a vision statement, and an organisation with a real sense of vision. In many cases, the reason for this difference is that the vision has been clearly and passionately communicated; this is vital if genuine commitment is to be gained for the vision. Key aspects of the vision message are:

Purpose – why the vision is so important
Picture – how things will look when the vision is achieved
Plan – how we are going to get there (strategic steps)
Part – that everyone has to play
Prompting – seeking feedback regularly

The vision message must be embedded into as many communication channels as possible, and personal contact is crucial to the vision promotion process. The vision leader needs to communicate the vision throughout the organisation at every opportunity. External communication of the vision is just as important as internal communication, and every opportunity must be taken to reinforce the vision message with key external stakeholders and influencers.

For instance, figure 44 illustrates how the technical team is meeting on May 25th. Areas for consideration in respect of reinforcing the new vision include having the vision statement automatically appearing on all emails, a new section on the company website, a VNR (video news release), podcasts and all business stationery (including business cards) to emphasise key messages.

The crucial elements of vision communication are:

One of the most effective methods of communicating the new vision is to have it associated with all new programmes and initiatives. Once the key goals are broken down into performance objectives, the vision can also be reinforced through reward systems. As indicated above, regular feedback sessions need to be held throughout the organisation; this is vital for monitoring progress and fine-tuning particular aspects of the vision.

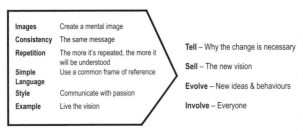

Whilst developing a detailed communication plan can require a significant time investment, even a brief outline (such as the extract above) can provide focus, establish a timetable, help set priorities, facilitate the identification of target audiences and key messages, and highlight the most appropriate communication methods. Communication plans can also help clarify aims, objectives, methods of evaluation and the resources required.

Vision Communication Plan—Busco Enterprises

Date	Venue	Target audience	Key message/activity	Method	Key figure(s)
May 20th	Conference room	Key internal & external stakeholder reps.	Their input highly valued (collective vision)	Discussion	The Board & target audience
May 21st	Conference room	Key internal & external stakeholder reps.	Producing the vision statement	Discussion	Executive team
May 22nd	Conference room	Dept. Managers	Delivering the vision	Briefing with Q & A session. Written pack	Executive team
May 23rd	Oak Hotel	Key internal & external stakeholders	What the new vision means to them	Presentation (refreshments)	Executive team
May 24th	Room 102	All customer-facing staff	Their part in realising the vision	Meeting with Q & A	Dept. Managers
May 25th	Operations room	Technical team	Reinforcing the vision (supporting media)	Team discussion	Operations manager
May 26th	Conference room	Local press	'The New Busco Vision'	Press conference	Executive team

Figure 44: Extract from a vision communication plan.

6.2 The Importance of trust

No matter how captivating the vision is, how good the product or service is, or how well the business is run, a company cannot function without trust. Trust between management and workers, trust between colleagues, trust between the company and its customers or clients, and trust in products and services are essential for the survival of any business. Where workers are concerned, trust is essential for gaining commitment rather than mere compliance. Trust is not a component of communication as such, nor is it a communication skill. Its importance lies in the fact that it is the *outcome* of the various aspects of communication behaviour considered throughout this book.

Perceptions of trust vary from person to person, organisation to organisation, and profession to profession. For example, an MORI poll found that doctors and teachers were trusted to the extent of 91% and 87%, respectively. However, journalists and politicians both scored just 18%. Interestingly, the same poll confirmed that honesty overrides factors such as product quality and customer care as the key indicator for judging business organisations.

The presence of trust gives organisations:

- Increased focus and vision
- A sense that aims and objectives will be reached
- Full co-operation in the interests of everyone
- Increased competitiveness
- The ability to implement change successfully
- The confidence to take business risks
- Customer loyalty

Trust can also be seen as a source of sustainable competitive advantage. Firstly, as the above indicates, its value lies in enabling the business to meet customer needs more effectively. Secondly, it leads to superior performance. Thirdly, because of its nature, it is more difficult for others to imitate and takes time to generate and grow.

Human beings are essentially social animals, and trust is a dimension of our dependence on each other to maintain fulfilling personal and working relationships. There are many definitions of trust, but simply stated, trust is the belief in the word, actions or decisions of another; and where required, the willingness to act on this belief. Trust is contextual and dynamic, it can grow or diminish over time.

Figure 45: The Circle at trust.

Trust can take different forms:

Self-trust – the confidence we have in our own ability and the personal and business judgements we have to make. This is essential for us to be able to do our jobs competently, and for getting others to trust us. Our willingness to trust others increases with our ability to trust ourselves.

Relational trust – this is the general trust one places in others; it forms over time as we come to experience the personality, character and judgement of others. Often, our trust is based on a number of elements such as our view of others' competence, their integrity, their past behaviour and how truthful we think they are

Expert trust – a specific type of trust that is generated by our confidence in a person's knowledge, skills, competence or training in a particular area

Structural trust – arises from the position that an individual holds. It is a form of trust that is associated with a company or institution, as well as the individual (we may know little about the individual, but have trust in the office he or she holds and the values attached to it)

Transactional trust – whilst this form of trust may be affected by some of the above factors, it is largely time related. It applies only in a particular context, and at a particular point in time (e.g., that another person will honour their word over a particular deal)

Communication Trust – This refers to the willingness to disclose relevant information; transparency between individuals and at all levels in an organisation is a vital element here. So, too, is being discrete and sensitive where personal information is concerned. Being truthful, admitting mistakes and giving honest feedback are other key components in building communication trust.

Building trust

Building trust means establishing and maintaining effective relationships, and exhibiting behaviour that is appropriate in this respect. Whilst trust can be established quickly through factors such as sharing a common set of values, being receptive to a person's communication style (that conveys they are trustworthy), or a specific incident that demonstrates that a person is to be trusted, trust is usually established over a period of time. Strong trust is normally the result of factors such as: being discrete, behaving fairly, keeping promises, being loyal and experiencing that others are acting in your best interests. Although all of the above are of vital importance, the core factors in establishing trust (especially in the business sense) can be seen to be competence, consistency, communication and integrity.

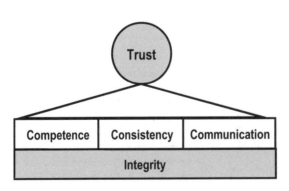

Figure 46: The foundations of trust.

Competence consists of possessing knowledge, skills and ability to a degree that generates confidence and trust. But competence also consists of being aware of one's limitations and exuding a 'quiet confidence' in one's capabilities. *Consistency* means responding in the same way, or making similar judgements when faced with the same circumstances (unless there is good reason not to do so). Essentially, consistency is about 'walking the talk'—matching words with deeds.

As indicated previously, *communication* is also a key trust builder, and important aspects here are openness, quality of communication, self-disclosure and frequency. Having an open communication style means not just being approachable, but also revealing as much information as you can in the circumstances. Openness also entails genuine listening and the establishment of a dialogue. As mentioned in Chapter One, quality communication means communication that is relevant, timely and meaningful to the individual. Appropriate self-disclosure between individuals builds a bond that strengthens mutual trust. Engaging in frequent communication builds trust levels, and makes communication more credible when problems occur.

Integrity is the bedrock of trust and means more than just being honest in the usual sense. It entails being totally honest in your dealings with others, and having the highest values and standards (and honouring these). All of the above form a 'credibility factor'; how much we can rely on others to act impartially, or in our best interests.

In a more general sense, achieving a reasonable degree of trust requires that we engage in trust-building behaviour. Sometimes, this entails practising the 'law of reciprocity'; we demonstrate trust in others in the hope that they will trust us in return. The importance of personal contact in the trust building process cannot be overestimated.

Trust undermined

Although trust can take a considerable time to be established, it can be undermined by one act or a number of incidents (these may be unrelated). Where trust is undermined by one incident, the breach of trust is usually the result of the seriousness of the particular incident. In the personal sense, trust can be undermined by things such as not keeping promises, betraying a confidence, complete self-interest and an unwillingness to trust others.

In the corporate sense, trust can be undermined by one or more of the following:

- Lack of a clear vision
- Lack of communication (or mainly, top-down communication)
- A culture of blame
- Internal competition
- Lack of feedback (or feedback given inappropriately)
- Reluctance to delegate
- Poor teamwork
- Decisions tend to be imposed

Lack of organisational trust creates an environment that is stressful and not as productive as it could be. At one level, the result could be poor customer relationships; at another, it can result in lack of competitiveness and business failure. Whether it occurs at a personal or organisational level, it must be remembered that mistrust is much more difficult to deal with than an absence of trust. Mistrust is not just the outcome of prior or current experiences, it is a combination of beliefs, perceptions and interpretations. Once established, these can be very difficult to overcome.

Rebuilding trust

Although it depends upon the particular circumstances, and it can be very difficult, it is sometimes possible to rebuild trust. Whether the breach of trust has occurred in a personal or an organisational setting, the strategy to restore trust is basically the same:

Personal	Organisational
Listen and respond to others	Create a shared vision
Act with discretion	Lead by example
Be consistent	Practise open communication
Invest - trust others	Promote shared values
Keep promises	Share responsibility - delegate
Be honest with others	Be loyal
Confide in others	Display competence
Accept responsibility	Act with integrity
Forgive mistakes	Share decisions

Figure 47: Summary of key trust builders.

1. Listen carefully to the person whose trust has been breached
2. Assume personal responsibility (trying to blame others will only make things worse)
3. Offer an immediate apology (explain the circumstances if relevant)
4. Make reparation (this will differ from case to case, re-read 'doing mode', page 35)
5. Give an assurance that it will not happen again (establish a procedure for this, and explain it)
6. Ask the person is there anything else you can do to rebuild trust

The best practice, of course, is not to breach trust in the first place, and this situation is best avoided by individuals and organisations focusing on the key trust-builders (figure 47).

An important factor in building trust that has not been referred to so far is motive. Motive in turn is linked to integrity; both are elements of character. When an individual's motive is not purely selfish, then trust will grow. Conversely, when the motive is based wholly on self-interest, mistrust usually follows.

Apart from significant experiences that produce an almost instant emotional response in terms of trust building, the complex nature of human relationships means that we cannot be sure how long trust will take to evolve (or whether it will occur at all). What we can be sure about is that trust is fragile, trust becomes stronger over time and trust has to be earned.

We can only find out whom to trust by taking risks. Sometimes the risks involve self-disclosure about issues that we would prefer to remain private, or within a small and intimate group of friends; sometimes our trust is betrayed. But it is always better to take the risk than to remain always distrusting of others. In distrusting others, we implicitly distrust ourselves.

6.3 Customer orientation

In recent years, organisations have been increasing focusing on customer relationship management (CRM). The basis of CRM is the production of customer information and the generation and managing of the relationship between the organisation and the customer base. Three distinct trends have emerged in relation to CRM: the production and analysis of information referred to above; supporting customers through sales and service representatives (or automation of this function); and direct communication with the customer.

As the comments on page 22 have previously confirmed, customer data can include factors like products purchased, contact history and potential profitability. This information is then used for purposes such as marketing campaigns, product decision-making, and financial forecasting. Unfortunately, although information lies at the centre of CRM, many companies tend to place the emphasis on analysing data and trends purely to generate more business; ensuring that the customer has had a good buying or service experience often takes second place. This state of affairs has led to the situation where there is, quite often, a serious mismatch between a business organisation's perception of the quality of their customer service, and the experience of their customers. Indeed, many businesses view customer service merely as a complaints-handling process, rather than a marketing and customer retention opportunity.

Evidence in this respect has emerged from a series of research findings. For example, recent research into technology companies by the Accenture organisation reveals that 58% of the customers surveyed rated the service they received as average or below average; 73% of customers were at risk of defecting. This was completely at odds with the view held by company executives: 75% held that their companies provided 'above average' customer service; 77% believed that self-service CRM systems had a positive impact on the business; and 93% of executives stated that CRM software led to speedier resolution of problems (this in turn led to higher customer satisfaction). Other customer views revealed that 42% had to access customer service channels many times in order to resolve their problem, 61% held that technology had not improved customer service, and only 13% stated that online self service was valuable.

The Accenture findings echo similar results from other research. For example, Harris Interactive research (again into technologies) found that 90% of customers had a negative customer service experience, and 53% experienced difficulty in getting help over the phone or through the web. Even if these research findings are not exactly confirmed by other consumer research, there is little doubt that a significant problem exists with respect to customer service.

This appears to be due to several reasons: the historical focus on cost reduction (excellent companies view customer service as an investment, not a cost), the automation of the customer care process, and the off-shoring of the customer care process (especially in the UK).

Cost reduction in relation to customer service is misplaced, since it is generally accepted in business that getting and selling to a new customer can cost much more than selling to an existing one. Similarly, a customer experiencing poor service will often tell others; this simply compounds the potential business loss. The automation of the customer service process has fled in the face of a basic communication principle; people would rather speak to another person than a machine. The frustration of speaking to recorded messages is only increased by being instructed to press what seems to be an interminable sequence of numbers. Such experiences are only multiplied when the customer service process is out-sourced to a foreign country. Some UK companies have re-located their customer service provision back in the UK, because the perceived cost reduction was outweighed by the increase in unhappy customers.

It is understandable that companies are concerned about high rates of calls to customer service centres. However, as long as the customer is left satisfied, high volumes of calls to service centres is not necessarily a bad thing. What needs to be done, however, is a wholesale analysis of *why* customers are calling; and along with this, an evaluation of what can be done to render the calls unnecessary in the first place.

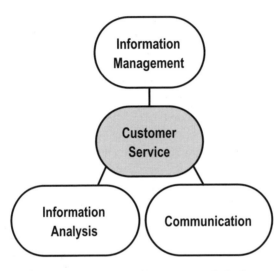

Figure 48: Information & communication aspects of effective customer service.

Despite the poor press that call centres receive, recent research by Genesys Telecommunications Laboratories found that 61% of respondents believed that call centres were doing a better job than three years ago. Importantly, the research also found that 75% of respondents would give more business to a company based on great contact experience. Like many other consumer surveys, this research confirmed that customer service is a critical driver of satisfaction, and thus, profitability.

Although it is good to see some call centres improving and meeting customer expectations in terms of service, at the same time, it must be remembered that customer expectations are rising. The Genesys research also revealed a rising trend towards methods of providing customer service other than traditional telephone-based call centres. Some 86% of consumers want email communication; indeed, 45% wanted email to become their primary method of customer service. In addition, 19% would prefer instant messaging (web chat), whilst 17% wanted SMS text. Furthermore, response times were critical, with 17% who preferred email wanting a response within four hours; 47% of those who preferred emails wanted a response within twenty-four hours.

What customers want

Apart from satisfaction concerning the product or service, an examination of customer expectations reveal that the following are not unusual:

- Giving and receiving information
- Courtesy and consideration

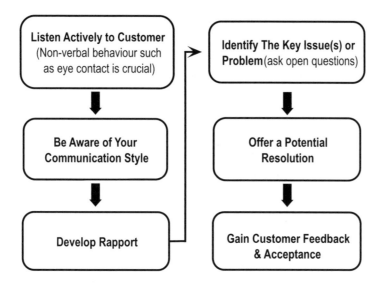

Figure 49: Resolving customer service problems—positive communication interaction.

- The exploration of options and alternatives
- Empathy
- A degree of control relating to the transaction

If the aspect of control related to the transaction is removed, then all the other factors are associated with after sales service. The factors are also inextricably linked to communication behaviour. Customer service, then, is not just about providing quality products and services, but also being aware of, and positively responding to, a whole range of communications and linked behaviours. In addition, effective communication between the business organisation and the customer also requires effective information analysis and information management.

What business organisations need to do

Many companies resent customers complaining, when this is in fact, a positive process. It is a positive process because it can highlight failures in the product, service, problem resolution process or employee training. Detailed analysis of the information generated from the customer service process, and subsequent management of this in terms of issue classification, are critical for customer retention.

Consequently, it is vital that companies focus not just on *efficiency* measurements (the cost per customer service contact or case), but also on *effectiveness* measurements (success rates and the time taken). Accordingly, companies should be more concerned about customers who have a service problem but do not complain, rather than those who do. Business organisations really need to understand the critical importance of customer service. Research confirms that:

- Only a small percentage of customers ever complain, most dissatisfied customers just do not return
- Unhappy customers are an important source of information about the business
- Many unhappy customers will return to the business if their problem is resolved

- The multiplier effect is very damaging; one unhappy customer will often tell several others
- It costs significantly more to attract a new customer, than to retain an existing one
- The lifetime value of a customer is worth a lot more than the odd customer return or cost of resolving an issue to the customer's satisfaction

In order to offer good customer service, companies need to:

- Provide relevant service information to customers, and analyse the information from them
- Be proactive about communicating
- Use a variety of communication channels (e.g., emails, SMS, instant messaging, interactive web sites, blogging)
- Conduct regular communication training
- Emphasise the importance of courtesy and active listening to service centre staff
- Retrain service centre staff who speak like robots
- Be flexible, and go for a win-win outcome (if the customer loses, so does the business)
- Treat 'internal customers' well (employees who are poorly treated often treat customers poorly)
- Put people first, technology second (identify what customer service problems require people contact)
- Refrain from making promises you cannot keep
- Focus on keeping customers rather than making sales (customer satisfaction builds loyalty, loyalty builds profits)

Apart from issues such as faulty products, negative buying experiences are almost always linked to poor customer service. It would seem, then, that there is some truth in the old business maxim, 'if you take care of the customer, the business takes cares of itself'. Many businesses can bring customers in, the real trick is to hold onto the ones you have and generate more. A company's quality of customer service defines who they are as a company.

Summary

- One of the most important concepts an organisation can communicate is its vision. Vision statements can reflect core values such as integrity, service, quality, social responsibility, excellence and innovation
- Those who are responsible for the envisioning process can be seen to go through three distinct stages: developing the vision, communicating the vision, and making the organisational changes necessary for the vision to be realised
- An organisation's mission statement is a vital part of its strategic plan, and its aim is to define the specific purpose of the business by capturing its goals and philosophy in a few sentences
- A business organisation cannot function effectively without trust: Trust between management and workers, trust between colleagues, trust between the company and its customers/clients, and trust in its products or services. Trust can also be seen as a source of competitive advantage

- Building trust means establishing and maintaining effective relationships, and exhibiting behaviour that is appropriate in this respect
- In recent years, business organisations have been increasingly focusing on customer relationship management (CRM). The basis of CRM is the production of customer information, and the generation and managing of the relationship between the organisation and the customer base
- A company's quality of customer service defines who they are as a company

Tutorial

1. Write out your personal or organisational vision:
   - how believable and realistic is it?
   - does it reflect your core values?
   - does anything need changing?
   - outline your action plan (how flexible is it?)
2. If your vision is an organisational one, how are you going to create buy-in? (e.g., what is your communication plan? how compelling is it?)
3. It is five years since your vision statement was first outlined, and most of your goals have been realised—describe the situation
4. What is your trust rating? (how you feel others trust you on a scale of 1–10)
5. If you have undermined the trust that others have placed in you, what is your trust recovery plan? (review pages 87 & 88)
6. Excellent customer service is mainly about generating and using information efficiently, and effective communication skills. Consequently:
   - Develop a system for analysing customer information
   - Using an organisation with which you are familiar, identify the main methods used for customer communication and draft an improvement plan
7. Using a business organisation of your choice, examine customer complaints for the last twelve months, are there common factors? If so, develop an effective strategy to overcome these
8. Draft a customer service policy designed to optimise customer loyalty

7 Maximising the business 2

One-minute overview

Public relations (PR) has sometimes been given a bad name, and sometimes, this has been deserved. However, practised in an ethical and professional manner, PR is one of the most useful marketing tools a business can have. PR consists of generating favourable publicity about the company and its products or services. The strength of PR lies in the fact that it is not paid-for publicity, since it operates mainly by attracting the interest of journalists and editors.

This chapter will enable you to:

- Understand the importance of PR
- Recognise the key elements of the PR process
- Appreciate the various forms that PR takes
- Be aware of how press releases are constructed
- Develop the knowledge and skills necessary for giving an effective media interview

7.1 Public relations

Along with promotions and personal selling, publicity is one of the most important marketing and selling mechanisms a business organisation possesses. Publicity consists of communicating in a planned and strategic manner, the key messages about an organisation and its products or services. Not only can publicity contribute in a significant way to enhancing a brand, but it can also do so at a lower cost. This is because it largely works through editors and journalists publishing or broadcasting the material as a newsworthy item, rather than a paid-for advertisement. This, of course, can increase its credibility from a public point of view.

The term Public Relations (PR) is somewhat misleading since public relations can relate to almost any activity that businesses engage in. Indeed, chapter eight is devoted to marketing communication, an activity that relates to business processes such as understanding buyer behaviour, advertising and sales promotion—all of these entail relations with the public. Whilst the term public relations is used in this chapter, its function is best understood in its original meaning of *press relations*.

PR is aimed at positively influencing a business organisation's brand or target audience. Originally, the difference between PR and other similar activities was that PR primarily achieved its aim through the editorial pages of the press, news or feature articles. Whilst journalists are still a vital vehicle in creating a positive image about the client's organisation or brand image, PR professionals now use a whole range of techniques from product launches and conferences, to the internet.

PR consultants are used for a variety of reasons: the organisation does not have its own PR expertise; to handle one-off assignments; to counter bad publicity.

PR can also play a part in attracting good quality employees, impacting favourably on share prices and creating an overall positive image of the business. Another way to view PR professionals is to see them as advocates for the business. Unfortunately, the modern practice of 'political spin' and the use of PR by celebrities and 'showbiz' personalities has created an image problem for the many highly professional PR consultants.

As indicated above, an important aspect of PR that sets it apart from other promotional activities (and heightens its impact) is that it is not directly paid-for advertising (with the exception of 'advertorials'—advertisements that adopt the style of a news item). The editorial screening process adds a degree of integrity that is often lacking from paid-for advertising. Conversely, the impact of PR is often not as immediate as paid-for advertising. Whereas paid-for advertising allows the advertiser to control the message, content and overall style, because PR is unpaid, its effect (and whether the story is aired at all) lies wholly in the hands of the particular editorial team (e.g., the magazine or newspaper). These aspects of PR emphasise the importance of the interest value of the story, and the fact that the more newsworthy it is, the greater the likelihood of it being promoted.

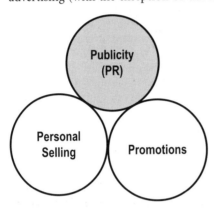

Figure 50: The three main generators of brand & image awareness.

PR stories tend to have a number of elements:

- The client input/brief
- The creative writing process
- The intended distribution group (e.g., editors and correspondents)
- Any particular angles or news slants

PR consultancies are used for a number of reasons: their expertise in translating and projecting an organisation's business objectives to a wider audience; the consultancy's contacts across a range of media vehicles; objectivity and an 'outside' view of the strong points of the business; practical experience in knowing what will work. Many businesses are unaware of the potential PR material they have, until it is highlighted by the PR professional.

The relationship between the client and the PR consultant is a crucial one, the client (known in PR terms as the 'account') contributing the information for the story and perhaps the marketing expertise; and the consultant who adds the particular news slant and the creative knowledge.

The expression, 'PR campaign', refers to a long and sustained PR effort. Unless a particular story is of sufficient magnitude, the best strategy is to use the 'drip effect'. Here, stories and articles are released over time in a planned manner that heightens impact. Though it takes more time, the added benefit of the PR campaign is that a more effective rapport is built up between the client and the target group.

The material for PR articles takes various forms, from product launches, new initiatives, significant contracts, specialist expertise (e.g., 'the only UK company to be able to…') and the appointment of new executives. In short, anything that has news value. However, there is a significant difference between something having news value and a successful news article; it is here that the PR professionals come into play and earn their fee.

As with all business processes, evaluation is an important activity, but how are PR initiatives evaluated? Useful yardsticks include the volume or extent of the coverage, increases in consumer enquiries or sales and the data gained from customer surveys. Another strategy is to compare the media coverage generated, with the equivalent cost of creating the same amount of advertising ('equivalent advertising value'). However, this does not measure the effectiveness of the PR initiative, just the equivalent cost of advertising. An effective PR campaign will generate a whole range of responses, from journalists and trades people, as well as the general public. All of these should be documented and examined, since they are important evidence indicators of PR effectiveness.

7.2 DIY PR

Although it is recommended that business organisations use PR experts when necessary, there are occasions when businesses may need to conduct the PR function themselves. Examples in this respect are when the cost may be prohibitive for a small business, or the matter requires an intimate knowledge that PR professionals may lack (e.g., the culture of the organisation), and cannot be gained in the time available.

Though many small to medium business enterprises would lack the expertise to make promotional tapes or videos, there are a number of PR activities that they could engage in, from writing copy to sponsorship, promotions, exhibitions and visits.

Sponsorship

Sponsorship can take a number of forms, from equipping the local football team, being involved with professional award schemes ('best regional finalist'), paying for advertising space, to supporting a community organisation such as a charity. The overriding reason for most sponsorship activity is the opportunity to communicate the name of the organisation, product or service to a wider audience. When this is done on a local or regional level, it has the added benefit of showing that the organisation is putting back something into the community. Sponsorship also achieves a number of other things: it helps generate goodwill and trust related to the business; it builds product or brand familiarity through repetition; and it creates the potential for further business (many people prefer doing business with those they are familiar with).

The decision to sponsor should entail a number of processes on the part of the business:

- Determining why they want to sponsor
- Evaluating all requests for sponsoring carefully
- Identifying business objectives
- Evaluating the sponsorship process regularly (e.g., have the business objectives been met?)

Promotions, functions and visits

As a PR tool, promotions and functions have become very effective; so much so, that it is unusual to find a good hotel without the facilities to stage such events. Activities under this heading can involve seminars, conferences and product launches.

Each potential venue needs to be evaluated, and a number of important questions need to be asked:

- Does the venue meet the overall needs of the activity?
- Is it conveniently located for most delegates?
- Does it have facilities for the disabled?
- Does it have appropriate accommodation if required?
- Are the technical facilities adequate (e.g., audio-visual aids)?

As with any such event, details are crucial, and matters like an outline programme of events (including workshops and keynote speakers) need to be attended to. Visits by VIPs such as the local MP, mayor or other local dignitary, are an ideal occasion to promote the business. This is especially so if the visit is linked to a business development like a new product or new premises. Visits also provide an ideal chance for a photo opportunity, thus consolidating the overall message (e.g., 'this business is successful').

Exhibitions

Even for large business organisations, organising an exhibition is very hard work. That's why many businesses seek to advance their cause by engaging in support activities like setting up an exhibition stand or engaging in PR activities at such a stand. Once again, a whole range of important activities need to be planned and executed proficiently. The old marketing adage, 'eye level is buy level' is particularly true where exhibitions and similar public events are concerned; people will judge the professionalism of the business by the standard they see at the event. Consequently, before the decision is made to attend an exhibition, a number of considerations need to be made:

- What are the business aims and objectives in relation to the exhibition?
- Will the exhibition convey the right image?
- How exactly will the exhibition advance our business?
- Can we justify the expense?
- How will we follow up our exposure at the exhibition?

In addition to ensuring that the overall image and presentation of the stand is of a high standard (and that there is sufficient quantities of promotional material, gifts bearing the company logo etc.), strategies with respect to optimising the media value of the event are crucial. These include contacting the exhibition press office *before* the event, identifying media opportunities such as press receptions, getting information about any visiting VIPs (can they visit your stand?) and maximising the number of personal contacts for follow-up activities.

Although producing press kits is a good idea, media representatives will be inundated with these. Therefore, the press kit needs careful design and presentation. Try to avoid content that is blatant advertising, and include material that is newsworthy (e.g., are there any interesting developments or new products? What is unique about your company? Has the company won any awards, important commissions or contracts?). Most importantly, most exhibitions have newsletters or daily bulletins; getting the business featured in these communication vehicles is a key priority. And finally, where exhibitions are concerned, keep a log of people who have visited your stand, or whom you have come in contact with. Their details are absolutely vital for any follow-up activity (events like exhibitions are a bit like planting seeds).

7.3 Press releases

Whether a press (news) release is being written on a DIY basis, or by a professional PR consultant, it is important for the small to medium business to understand its importance, its construction and its many uses.

A press release is a word-processed pseudo news story that contains information about the benefits of the business, its products, services or a newsworthy event. However, if the piece reads like an advertisement, it is unlikely to be published.

The intention of the press release is to grab the attention of an editor or journalist. Journalists are inundated with press releases, and the challenge is to appeal to the interests of the editor or publication by producing a piece that is innovative, newsworthy and of current interest. The newsworthy element is best understood by the writer putting themselves in the position of the reader; Why would they be interested? What's new or interesting about the piece? Why is it different? Another way to determine whether something is newsworthy or not is to assess how many of the target audience might be affected by the information or event, how many of them will need to know and, most importantly, how many will *want* to know.

Pieces that have a link to national stories or concerns, or offer an innovative business solution (the 'news hook'), have a greater chance of being published. In addition to audience considerations and the content itself, very often the answer lies in the way in which the piece is structured and written.

The conventional view is that press releases should be relatively short, anything from three to five hundred words. However, the real driver of story length should be the media vehicle that will carry the story. For example, a newspaper will probably prefer short stories, whereas a specialist or trade magazine might want much longer copy. Whatever length the final story is, it is best to use the 'topic sentence first' approach; in other words, get the key points early in the story, and the supporting detail later in the structure.

In addition to 'PRESS RELEASE' appearing in capitals at the head of the piece (usually centred), key components of the press release are:

The letterhead or company logo – this is a key marketing tool

The source of the press release – crucial details like the name and address of the company, telephone numbers etc.

The contact – this is the writer's name and contact details, and can lead to further media contact such as interviews (this can appear at the end)

Dates – these consist of the date the piece is being sent and, crucially, the date the piece is to be released. If a specific release date is required, this must be flagged up to the editor, otherwise, the release date is usually stated as 'FOR IMMEDIATE RELEASE' (release dates are in capital letters and usually placed at the left hand side).

Headline – although most editors will prefer their own headline, this is an important element of the piece and sets the press release in context. As with the style of the whole piece, the headline must grab attention. A headline like, 'Mike Scott, a local man wins important contract,' will have less of a chance of grabbing attention than, 'Surrey man impacts on world market'

Main body – here, the supporting details are given

If using more than one page, 'continued' should be clearly marked at the bottom of the preceding page. When the end of the piece is reached, this is normally signified by writing—END- in capitals (or # # #, depending upon the region or style requirements). After the end of the press release, brief details can be given about the company, e.g.

'Founded in 1980 by Mike Scott, Scott Engineering is a Surrey based company with strong roots in the local community. Scott uses environment-friendly materials, and where possible, all materials are sourced in the UK. Scott's apprenticeship scheme has won an Engineering Federation award, and the company gained the Queen's Export Award in 2006. Mike Scott was made an OBE in March 2007.'

After structure, the most important element of the press release is writing style. As indicated above ('topic sentence first'), journalists tend to 'write in reverse'; that is, they state the key point at the beginning and then add the detail and supporting evidence. This technique is illustrated by the 'inverted pyramid' (figure 51). Journalists also tend to adopt the KISS approach (Keep It Short & Simple); this means short sentences and short paragraphs. It is vital to avoid jargon, clichés and long-winded prose. The first paragraph or two should answer questions posed by the 5WH approach. The supporting detail may well include quotes from customers or leading figures in the particular field. Most importantly, press releases are written in the 'third person' or reported speech (e.g., instead of 'I found out', 'Research revealed that…'). Some editors prefer double spacing so that they can edit more easily, it is therefore important to make such notes on your contact list.

Producing press releases for email publishing is a growing trend, and a number of factors are responsible for this. Firstly, more and more people are using online sources to locate information on organisations, products and services. Secondly, the email can cut out 'middlemen' like editors and journalists and reach the target audience directly. Thirdly, advances in technology mean that a well-written news release (particularly with perceptive use of key words) can be boosted to the top of news search engines within twenty-four hours (technology can also allow you to track the response to your news piece by measuring the number of 'clicks'/'hits'). Fourthly, the PR value of the news release can be optimised by directing the reader to your website.

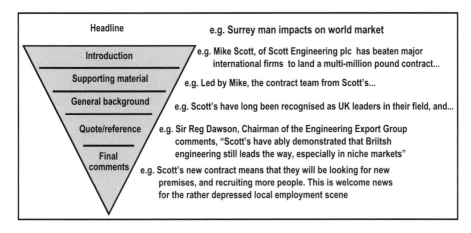

Figure 51: The inverted pyramid.

Email-designed press releases follow basically the same structure and style as traditional pieces, but some aspects differ:

- Email press releases tend to be shorter than traditional formats (an average of 500 words)
- Most journalists prefer plain text (avoid forced page breaks and tabs)
- Some recipients avoid opening attachments since they could contain a virus
- Remember to include your website link
- Always provide non-electronic contact details for journalists who may have limited on-line access
- Sending the piece in Rich Text Format can be useful, but check this with potential recipients
- Check that any photos etc. conform to the technical requirements of the recipients (e.g., high resolution)
- Although contact details and further information about the company are preferred after the—END-of the piece, in email releases, these can be obscured by advertising

The press release checklist ✓

- Be clear about the target audience
- Ensure its newsworthy (e.g., linked to a current event or media interest)
- If the piece has a limited link to news events, adopt the problem/solution strategy
- Specify a release date (in capitals)
- Make it easy for journalists (adopt the 5WH approach)
- Develop an attention-grabbing headline
- Pay attention to structure and style
- Put the key information first (inverted pyramid)
- Use active, not passive voice
- Keep the language simple and avoid hype or a selling strategy
- Ensure you cover copyright and permission issues (e.g., using quotes, referring to others)

- Go for the personal touch, and avoid using labels (traditional press releases)
- Check everything carefully (spell-checkers alone are not enough)

And finally, where press releases are concerned, a reminder that there are lots of opportunities for newsworthy events: new products, new staff, new approaches (innovation), a significant contract or expansion, sponsorship/supporting the community and links to an issue of regional or national importance.

7.4 The Media interview

It is true that media interviews involve losing a certain amount of control on the part of the interviewee. However, viewed positively, the media interview can be a win/win situation for both parties. On one hand, the journalist has their agenda of gaining the relevant facts about an issue of interest, balancing opposing views, and, where possible, to get quotes from a key source. On the other, the interviewee can obtain important exposure for their organisation or service, or be established as an expert whose views are to be considered seriously in any debate of relevance to their field. Nevertheless, it is important to recognise that the media in general are more concerned with meeting the needs of their public than promoting the particular needs of any organisation or product. It is, for this reason, that the promotional value for the interviewee is often implicit, rather than expressed.

Journalists work in a very competitive, time-constrained environment. For example, radio and television journalists have less time to produce stories than those who work for magazines. Often, the stories for radio and television are embarked upon in the morning, for broadcast that evening. Therefore, anyone who can understand and meet journalistic needs maybe called upon regularly to act as subject matter experts. Again, this is a win-win situation for the interviewee; a strong media contact list can be established and called upon when help is needed in return.

Journalists are especially interested in issues that fall under the following headings or guidelines:

Currency   An issue or event that is of current or immediate interest

Celebrity   The more well-known the person is, the greater the interest (e.g., 'MP suspended from party')

Conflict   Any situation where they may be a winner or loser, or heated public debates

Cliff-hangers   Situations where the outcome is awaited with suspense

Locality   A local link heightens the news value

Emotion   A whole range of situations that generate strong feelings

Scandal   The 'bad news is good news' approach

Whilst detailed general advice will be given in a separate section for all media, relevant comments will be made below where appropriate to particular medium.

Of all the media, television interviews can be particularly stressful for the inexperienced. Television interviews present their own challenges because, although the filming may last for fifteen or twenty minutes, only ten to twenty seconds will probably be shown. The secret is to speak in short, concise statements using the sound bite technique. It is often said that if you get a telephone call from a researcher or producer, the call is, in fact, your audition. Consequently, it is useful to have a series of 'takes' or views on particular topics, and a good overall command of your specific field.

Non-verbal behaviour (review pages 46 & 47) is especially important where television is concerned, and can add to or undermine the credibility of the message. Always look directly at the interviewer

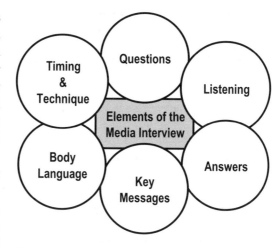

Figure 52:

(the camera will find you), and maintain firm eye contact. A good strong posture is important and gestures should be kept under control (e.g., moving hands or arms quickly can detract from impact, and folded arms can indicate defensiveness). A straight posture along with formal clothes can significantly add to your overall image and credibility. Unless it is inappropriate (e.g., a very serious topic), a smile can go a long way to indicate confidence, help cope with difficult questions and offset nervousness.

Whilst appearing on television may be flattering and large audiences can be reached, other media such as print and radio are not to be underestimated. The newspaper interview appears less pressured, and a good rapport can be established with the journalist; therein lies the danger. It is all too easy to drop one's guard and reveal something that is best left unsaid. As far as many journalists are concerned, there is no such thing as 'off the record', and this important issue needs clarification before the interview starts. Print journalists in particular like a good quote, so if possible, generate a few memorable phrases that neatly encapsulate the matter in hand. If the issue is a serious one with potential ramifications, it may be a good idea to record your comments, or have a friend or colleague with you. Claims that one has been misquoted may ring hollow unless you have evidence.

Radio, whether local or national, should never be underestimated as a powerful tool to communicate news, views or advocate issues. Based on careful demographic research of their potential audiences, radio stations have developed a number of interesting formats that allow effective targeting of relevant news and views. 'Breakfast shows', drive-time talk shows, tea-time formats and mobile studios have resulted in radio stations being even closer to current events and the development of new themes. The expansion of UK local radio stations has meant that people do not have to be famous or a celebrity to be heard, and 'local' stories can sometimes receive national media coverage.

When being interviewed on radio, try to get some indication of the potential questions you will be asked on air (this is good practice for all media). If you are not familiar with the particular show, try to find out the format (e.g., news, easy listening, large female audience); this will help you target the message better and use appropriate evidence. Using descriptive language is crucial for radio, and those interviewees that can 'paint a picture' in easily understood words will be asked back again. Most radio interviews are conducted over the phone, so a quiet room and a landline (avoid mobiles if possible) are essential. Cue cards with key points are also useful, but avoid simply reading out the words (writing for speaking is totally different from writing for reading).

The internet has become increasingly accepted as a key source of news and views, and presents new challenges to those who may wish to take advantage of this growing communication medium. Although such media give the 'broadcaster' more control over the message, a crucial aspect here is the particular site any potential item may appear on. Regular checks also need to be made to ensure that offensive items are not added to the site chosen for personal, company or product promotion. Developing expertise such as producing podcasts and website construction is essential for optimising the many opportunities that the internet offers.

Media interviews—general advice

Pre-interview groundwork

In addition to the comments above concerning television, radio, newspapers and the internet, pre-interview groundwork includes finding out exactly what the interview will be about, how long it will be, what form it will take (e.g. live, taped, one-to-one, if it's a radio interview, will the audience be phoning in with questions?), who the interviewer is and what type of audience you will be pitching to. Think carefully about giving impromptu interviews; if they value your input, they will wait until you are properly prepared. Indeed, an interview may not be the best form of response, and a carefully prepared statement may be more appropriate in the circumstances.

A vital part of any media interview is the decision about whether to get involved in the first place. The strategy here is to assess a range of issues; not the least, the PR opportunity. Examples of key questions in this respect are:

- What's the journalist's angle?
- Do I have the subject knowledge?
- What are the positive and potentially negative aspects?
- What do I want to achieve?
- How strong do I feel about the issue(s)?
- Will I be speaking on my own behalf, on behalf of the organisation or the field in general?

Interview preparation

Both interviewer and audience want an interview that is informative, positive and interesting. The interviewee can meet this remit by careful preparation, being knowledgeable about the matter under discussion, using simple language and an economy of words, and speaking *to* the interviewer rather than at them. Addressing these needs means careful and thorough preparation.

A vital part of the preparation process is to develop your strategy for the interview. This involves identifying the key points you want to make (three to five key points will form the basis of your overall 'message'). Although journalists may indicate some of the questions that may be asked, it is always best to anticipate a range of questions you might be asked, and generate appropriate responses. One of the best weapons an interviewee has is evidence (e.g., facts and figures). However, it is crucial to keep up to date on the relevant issues; one simple mistake regarding a fact or statistic can seriously undermine credibility.

Research is also important in respect of opposing views, since it is difficult to make your case if you do not understand the counter arguments. Planning *how* you are going to say something is just as important as what you say. The more you practise your interview, the better it will be on the day.

During the interview

No matter how good the preparation has been, the interviewee only has a second or two to answer. This means that active listening is crucial (review pages 58 & 59). For example, what does the question actually mean? Is it a 'booby trap' question?. If the question is unclear or ambiguous, ask for clarification ("do you mean…"). Difficult questions should be answered in a positive manner, and there are a number of techniques for coping with these; one of these is 'bridging'. In addition to helping the interviewee cope with a difficult question, the bridging technique also allows the interviewee to link their message to the question asked. For instance:

Question "Isn't it true that your company website failed to operate for five hours yesterday, and this caused considerable inconvenience to your customers?"

Bridge "Our website was shut down as part of a planned procedure because there was a perceived threat to security"

Message "We apologise for any inconvenience, but *we take our customers confidential details very seriously, and we have a duty to protect them*"

Another version of the 'bridge' technique is the ABC approach (Acknowledge, Bridge and Communicate). A key aspect here is to accept the negative part of the question, but balance this by the bridge and the communication. For example:

Acknowledge "Yes, it is true that we made 150 people redundant six months ago"

Bridge "But this was to protect the jobs of the majority of our workers after a world slump in the industry"

Communicate "Our order book is now full for the next five years, and all the workers made redundant have the opportunity to return on their existing terms and conditions"

Questions can also take the inverted pyramid structure, with a gentle lead-in and the 'killer question' coming last in the sequence of questions (review pages 57 & 58). Again, there are techniques for responding to the killer question. Examples in this respect are: *"Yes, but an even more important point is…"*; *"But that's not the critical issue, the critical issue is…"*; *"That's one view of course, but in these circumstances, I believe most people will…"*

Keeping control of the interview means the interviewee not just being confident and assertive, but also not accepting unfair interpretations or negative paraphrasing. The following sequence is an illustration in this respect:

Journalist "How do you explain the rise in anti-social behaviour in the county?

Interviewee   "There are a variety of causes for young people behaving anti-socially, what happens in the home is a significant factor"

Journalist   "So you're saying that parents are responsible"

Interviewee   "No, I'm not. What I am saying is that parents have an important role to play in reducing misbehaviour. For example, in three centres in the county, parents are currently working with youth and community leaders to set up intervention strategies"

Journalist   "Surely this is wishful thinking and will cost a fortune"?

Interviewee   "Wishful thinking, it's not. Malicious damage and complaints about misbehaviour are down by 25% across the three areas in question (**point 1**). When one considers that the cost of malicious damage claims met by the council in these three areas alone amounted to £100,000, this is in fact a saving of £25,000 (**point 2**). In addition, the cost of the project is being met by the Home Office (**point 3**); so this is a win-win situation all round" (a memorable phrase)

The above responses are not just illustrations of refusing to accept negative paraphrasing, but also indicate the techniques of sequencing the answer in such a way that adds to the impact of the response; using evidence very effectively; and getting the key messages across (misbehaviour is a serious problem; the council is taking a lead in tackling it; the community needs to work together; attempts to tackle the problem are successful and cost effective).

The Media interview checklist ✓

In addition to the recommendations already made, giving successful media interviews entails:

- Staying calm, confident, focused and 'on message'
- Speaking to be understood, rather than to impress (use simple words and avoid jargon)
- Less is more—the less you say, the greater the impact (answer questions briefly)
- Making your voice interesting—vary pitch and tone
- Using evidence effectively
- Displaying positive non-verbal behaviour (even on radio, a smile adds to the voice)
- Using analogies and examples to aid understanding
- Avoiding 'no comment' responses (it gives the impression that you have something to hide)
- Developing a list of good practice or top tips (journalists and audiences really like these)
- Not answering hypothetical questions
- Finishing on a memorable note where possible (known in the trade as a 'good out')

Now firmly established as part of the marketing mix, public relations is a key promotional technique. Brand and company-related features across the various media help to establish and maintain the market image of products, services, organisations and people. In a rapidly changing business environment, PR needs to be quick in execution, flexible and cost effective. No matter what form it takes, successful PR is essentially about thought leadership: communicating a strategic vision to others in an informative and compelling manner.

Summary

- Publicity is one of the most important marketing and selling mechanisations a business organisation possesses. Public relations (PR) consists of communicating in a planned and strategic manner, the key messages about an organisation and its products and services
- One of the strengths of PR is that it is not directly paid-for advertising
- Although many small to medium enterprises would lack the expertise to make promotional tapes or videos, they can engage in PR activities such as writing copy, sponsorship, promotions, exhibitions and visits
- A press release is a word-processed pseudo news story that contains information about the benefits of the business, its products, services or a newsworthy event. The purpose of the press release is to grab the attention of editors and journalists
- A useful framework for writing press releases is the inverted pyramid. This represents the structure where the key point is stated at the beginning and the supporting details and evidence follow
- The media interview presents an ideal opportunity for promoting the business. Preparation for the interview is vital and entails: identifying the key points you want to make (your 'message'); identifying any potentially difficult questions; and reviewing the 'ABC' answering technique (page 102)
- In a rapidly changing business environment, PR needs to be quick in execution, flexible and cost effective. No matter what form PR takes, it is essentially about thought leadership; communicating a strategic vision to others in an informative and compelling way

Tutorial

1. Public relations is *not* direct advertising. Outline the PR strategy you would adopt to draw attention to a company's new product.

2. A client has no previous experience of media exposure, but will be interviewed shortly by a TV presenter about a serious systems failure (this affected hundreds of customers). Outline the advice you would give to the client.

3. Senior executives in a company are considering developing links with a PR agency. Draft a list of criteria and key questions that would help them reach a decision.

8 Maximising the business 3—marketing communication

One-minute overview

No matter how good the product or service might be, they seldom sell themselves. Whereas in the history of business competition, one or two products might have dominated the market, an ever-growing number of products and services compete for market share. This situation is compounded by an age of increasingly intensive business competition and the internationalisation of markets. It is within this context that market communications assumes a critical position. Using a variety of communication tools such as advertising and sales promotion, market communicators seek to obtain maximum focus on the benefits of the particular product or service

This chapter will enable you to:

- Understand the role of marketing communication
- Realise the need for integrating the marketing communication process
- Appreciate the importance of understanding buyer behaviour
- Understand the need for media planning
- Identify the various communication tools that are available
- Be aware of the reasons for particular media vehicle decisions

8.1 A Brief overview of marketing

When mass production first developed, many business organisations produced goods and services with the hope that they would be purchased. This situation was best illustrated by Henry Ford's famous dictum that customers could have any colour they wanted as long as it was black. The introduction of marketing brought the important element of planning to the whole process of identifying, anticipating and meeting customer requirements. However, although marketing was recognised as an important business function by the late 1950s, the emphasis was placed almost wholly on advertising and promotion. Consequently, marketing departments tended to operate separately, their strategic significance was recognised by few organisations until the onset of the intense competition and increased consumer awareness of the 1980s and 90s.

The renewed focus on marketing meant that making profits was not the only objective for business organisations. Brand awareness, market share and customer retention became the goals of the modern business organisation. Thus, the short-term focus on profit creation alone was replaced by the long-term concentration on the customer as a generator of market dominance and long-term business success.

A strategic marketing approach places the customer at the centre of the business process and entails:

- Identifying customer needs
- Developing the product or service to meet the defined need
- Ensuring right product, right place, right time, right quantities and right price (the 5Rs)

Marketing is often referred to as consisting of the 4Ps: Product, Price, Place and Promotion. However, in reality, there are actually 6Ps, with the additional key elements being People and the marketing Process itself. The communication aspect of marketing is referred to as the marketing mix, and this consists of aspects such as: corporate identity, sales promotion, advertising, selling, public relations and publicity. Additional aspects not to be forgotten are areas like packaging, point of sales, exhibitions, sponsorship, and, of course, the internet. Figure 53 illustrates how the communication mix impacts the marketing mix. The fact that people change, markets change, technology changes and the nature of competition itself changes, highlights the crucial role that marketing communication plays in such a dynamic environment.

Figure 53:

8.2 Integrated marketing communication (IMC)

The role of marketing communications is to communicate the benefits of a product or service. IMC is a concept or strategy that combines all aspects of marketing communication such as advertising, sales promotion, public relations and direct response. Its overall objective is to create and convey a single marketing message through all aspects and stages of a campaign. Such an approach embraces all related elements from packaging, promotions and pricing, through to distribution. A *really* integrated approach to marketing communication will also cover aspects like the corporate mission, employee training and customer service. An important aspect of IMC is that each element of the communication mix should complement each other, thus producing a single unified message.

There are a number of reasons for the shift towards an integrated approach to marketing communications. These include:

- The growth in different forms of media advertising (e.g., the internet)
- The fundamental shift in market control (from a largely manufacturing-dominated market to a market that is dominated by retailers and consumers)
- The rise of data-based marketing (supplanting general-focus advertising)
- The growth of specialised media that enables better targeting of key groups

Nevertheless, despite the sense that IMC makes, there are a number of obstacles. Foremost among these is the human one. By their nature, marketers are creative people, and therefore, opinions will vary as to what is the best media vehicle for a particular message. Another example in this respect is the different views that marketers have regarding the general approach to advertising. Some marketers prefer advertisements that have a maximum breadth of appeal (a series of ads with a cumulative impact). Others opt for depth of appeal (ads that contain within them, the maximum number of awareness-raising, brand-linked and motivational points). It is within these circumstances that market research plays a crucial part, providing the evidence that helps resolve such conflicts.

Understanding the target market and buyer behaviour is fundamental to developing a marketing communication strategy. Whilst these issues have been briefly referred to earlier (page 22), further consideration is essential for understanding marketing communication. Once again, elements of the 5WH criteria come into play:

Aspect	**Dimension**
Attention	– Cognitive
Interest	– Affective
Desire	– Affective
Action	– Action

Figure 54: Understanding.

a. Who is the buyer? (understanding the target market)

b. Why do they buy, or prefer a particular product or brand?

c. How, when and where do they buy?

It is much easier to identify the answer to *a* and *c*, than *b*, since the answer to *b* involves a complex mix of motives; these range from impulse buying to rational consideration. In short, different market segments buy for different reasons, at different points in time. Nevertheless, consumer choice can be strongly influenced by trust in the product or brand name, advertising or promotion.

The old marketing adage of the 5Rs (page 107) highlights other important factors in buyer behaviour. For example, one leading UK supermarket chain lost a significant percentage of the market through not having products on the shelves. The market communicators had done their job, since customers were already sold on product, quality and price. Thus, the marketing *communication* mix worked, but elements of the marketing mix failed.

Although the AIDA model (figure 54) is used in fields other than buying behaviour (e.g., personal or professional development), E K Strong's 1925 acronym is a simple device for illustrating the cognitive, affective and behavioural dimensions of buyer behaviour. Whilst such 'response hierarchy'

Mini Glossary	
Cognitive	The process of gaining knowledge including perception, intuition and reasoning
Affective (domain)	Concerned with values and feelings. Also relates to how we perceive, interpret and respond to others

models are useful for prioritising communication objectives (i.e., whether a cognitive, affective or behavioural response is required), it is important to realise that not all buyers go through the above stages; or, indeed, in the sequence indicated. In addition, market communicators may wish to focus on particular aspects highlighted by the model, such as changing buyer desire.

Marketing communication is composed of a number of elements that help in understanding and influencing buyer behaviour. Key aspects here are beliefs, attitudes, standards and intentions. Other important considerations are the role of human perception, the learning process and motivation. The saying, 'keeping up with the Jonses' highlights the additionally important factors of social prestige and group influence. Any marketing communication strategy is only as good as the intelligence it is based upon. Key criteria in this respect is illustrated by the information given in figures 55 and 56.

In order for a marketing communicating strategy to be successful then, marketing communicators need:

- Relevant and accurate information about buyer beliefs and desires
- A clear understanding of what motivates consumers to buy
- Information on how individuals might perceive product brands and images
- Information on aspects such as income and lifestyles
- An intrinsic understanding of the product's unique selling points (USPs)

Whilst it is difficult for the marketing communicator to weave their way through the complex web of what influences buyer behaviour, there are notable successes. Recent UK successes include the Jamie Oliver campaign for Sainsburys, and the adoption of female fashion icons for Marks and Spencers (AGIL factors were crucial here). Notwithstanding, there have also been notable failures. An early and classic example of a marketing communications failure was the 1959 television campaign for Strand cigarettes. The TV advertisement consisted of a man in an overcoat and hat looking suitably serious and smoking a cigarette. The slogan accompanying the image was, 'You're never alone with a Strand'. Unfortunately, consumers associated the brand with loneliness.

Age
Gender & geography
Income
Lifestyle

Figure 55: Key market intelligence factors.

The Strand cigarette advertisement illustrates an important marketing communication principle: it is the *total* communication package, not just one element (such as image) that leads to success. The real challenge for marketing communicators lies not just in the collation of information about factors that influence buyer behaviour, but interpreting these correctly, understanding the product's USPs, and pitching the message in a meaningful and appropriate way.

Station	Social Class				Gender		Age					
	AB	C1	C2	DE	Men	Women	16–24	25–34	35–44	45–54	55–64	65+
BBC 1	19	26	18	37	43	57	6	11	16	17	20	31
BBC 2	19	24	18	39	47	53	5	10	13	15	20	37
ITV 1	13	22	20	44	38	62	6	10	15	17	19	33
Ch. 4/C4C	17	25	19	38	43	57	12	16	18	16	14	24
Five	14	20	19	47	42	58	9	14	18	16	18	25
Others	16	27	22	35	48	52	13	18	23	18	15	12

Figure 56: TV audiences by social class, gender and age (figures given in percentages). Source: BARB July 'o7

The above social class categories relate to the Registrar General's classifications and are often used by advertisers. The details are as follows:

A: Higher managerial, professional and administrative

B: Middle management, professional and administrative

C1: Supervisory, clerical and junior management

C2: Skilled manual workers

D: Semi and unskilled manual workers

E: Pensioners, casual workers and the unemployed

8.3 Media planning

The internet is just one example of the many new opportunities for marketing communications that now exist. Although brief references may be made to the internet, this will be examined in detail later. Consequently, this section will refer to traditional media vehicles like press, television, radio, direct mail and telemarketing.

Even when the decision as to what particular media is to be used is reached, further decisions remain; these include aspects such as where in the particular media should the message appear, and how often should it be reinforced. Therefore, media planning is an important part of marketing communication. Other considerations also impact media planning. For instance, most of the budget goes on the media vehicle, rather than the creative or production process.

A key tenet of media planning is maximum coverage at minimum cost. In order to make the crucial decisions associated with media planning, many marketing communicators commission audience research. Significant questions arise here too, like what influence does the particular media vehicle have on the target group, and how often is the particular media used? Among other issues to be considered is, what is best: a short concentrated burst, or the drip effect?

Even allowing for those viewers who make the tea during advertisements, television still has a large 'captive' audience. In addition, the passive nature of television viewing can create a particularly receptive consumer environment. An idea of the vast revenue associated with television advertising can be gained from Unilever's decision to cut their television budget during the years 2000–2005. The decision to reduce their television budget by 20% resulted in £60 million being removed from the UK total television advertising market during the period in question.

Unilever's decision to reduce their TV advertising budget was also a sign of the growing shift towards 'relationship' advertising campaigns. The objective here is to create

Media Planning – Important Considerations

Cover/reach	– number of the target audience reached by the media vehicle (%)
Particular social group	– target audience
Frequency	– the number of times an advertisement is placed
Exposure rate	– the number of times the target audience has the opportunity to see the particular advertisement
Cost per thousand (CPT)	– the average cost of reaching 1,000 of the population

Figure 57:

a long-term relationship with the consumer. As mentioned earlier, this in itself mirrors the shift in focus from short-term profit generation alone to a more long-term view of the customer as a generator of market dominance and business success. A very good example of relationship marketing is the sponsorship by Flora of the London Marathon.

Although the cost of TV ads can vary from £10,000 to £300,000, the CPT is relatively low. Peak time and national exposure can add significantly to the cost. Nevertheless, for many companies and organisations, the relatively high cost of TV commercials is seen as good value. A case in point was the 2006 UK 'Remember a Charity TV campaign' devised by Target Direct. The TV commercial featuring Michael Buerk, along with a press advertising campaign and in-house PR drive, resulted in the recognition rate of the charity's slogan ('Everyone can leave the world a better place') increasing from 38% to 49% among the 45-plus age group. In addition, the number of adults surveyed during the period in question who stated that they were 'very' or 'fairly' likely to leave something in their will, increased from 22% to 26%.

The cost break-down for Target's campaign was £205,000 for the TV commercial and £77, 470 for the press ad element. Given the fact that in the UK, every 1% rise in the number of people who leave legacies results in £100 million per year coming into the charity sector, this campaign can be seen to be very good value for money.

Direct response television marketing (DRTV), where the format of the advertisement entails direct marketing techniques, has become a major growth area, with a 25% share of the total TV advertising market. The interactive nature of DRTV usually involves the viewer being prompted to contact the advertiser by telephone or to visit the advertiser's web site. Consequently, the objective is to elicit an immediate response from the viewer.

Although the growth of regional radio, along with radio market segmentation (e.g., Radio 1, Radio 2, Radio 4), has allowed for better targeting of the marketing communication message, the effectiveness of the message can be diluted by the fact that listening to the radio is largely a 'background' activity. Nevertheless, in terms of outlay, production costs and CPT are relatively low. The effect of radio advertising is best optimised when it is used in conjunction with other media.

As with other media, radio advertising is based on the key premise of repetition. However, whilst repetition in some media can wane over time (e.g., newspapers), radio advertising can actually result in increased response rates. An important consideration here is air time; media experts recommend that, to be effective, radio ads need to be heard a minimum of three times per week. In contrast to production costs being relatively low, airtime can prove expensive. A simple twenty second ad broadcast by a small station will cost between £200–£300. The same ad by a London radio station can cost up to ten times this amount.

Whether national or regional, an important fact about newspapers is that they are purposely chosen. This means that the consumer is proactively engaged with the medium, and usually trusts it. An additional, positive factor about newspapers is that it is more easy to target specific consumer groups. This is particularly so, since many newspapers now contain daily and weekend supplements that appeal to particular genders, lifestyles or socio-economic groups. Whilst the cost of production and CPT varies from low to medium, an important cost factor is the specific nature of the advertisement and where it appears in the newspaper (and which newspaper).

It is true that newspaper circulation is falling, but despite this fact, the medium has a number of positive features:

- 36 million people read a national newspaper every week
- Whereas media like radio and TV are passively embraced, reading newspapers is an active process
- Newspapers have a permanent 'message' (they can be referred to again and again)
- Approximately 19,000 pages of business editorials are produced by national newspapers yearly
- Newspapers play an important part in directing consumers to websites
- Final copy can be delivered at short notice (greater flexibility for advertisers)
- Newspapers are considered the prime advertising medium by 99.4% of retailers
- Newspapers are more cost effective than TV

In contrast to other media vehicles like TV, newspapers represent a cost effective advertising tool for small businesses. For instance, a quarter page ad in a local newspaper will cost about £800. Even at a national level, the comparative good value of newspaper advertising is evident. Indeed, the Newspaper Marketing Agency (NMA) announced that the national newspaper's share of the UK display ad market rose to 14% in 2007 (figures compiled by Nielsen Media Research). An important factor in the increase was the NMA finding new revenue-generating sectors such as food and cosmetics.

As with newspapers, magazine readers deliberately choose their media vehicle. Key features of this medium are:

- Almost 80% of UK consumers read a magazine
- Most readers are likely to be in a relaxed mood
- Magazines are targeted at specific lifestyles, social groups and gender
- The production costs are low to medium; the CPT is medium

Therefore, marketing communicators can effectively target specific consumer groups. Even within traditional media like newspapers and magazines, other communicating methods can be used. Examples in this respect are leaflet inserts, reader offers and promotions.

Other traditional media such as posters and direct mail are also important considerations for the marketing communicator. Posters are aimed at passers by, such as pedestrians and those travelling in vehicles. Their impact can greatly depend upon the nature of the advertisement; so too can their costs. An important element here is, where the poster is sited; the more prestigious the site, the greater the cost. Though the production costs of direct mail are low, the CPT can be quite high. In addition, unsolicited direct mail can alienate some consumers, and generate complaints.

The following statistics are an indication of the media preferences for UK marketing communicators:

- The press (newspapers, magazines and directories) accounted for the largest share of total advertising expenditure at 45% (including production)
- Television: 25.4%
- Direct mail: 12.5%
- The internet: 7.5% (up from 4.5% in 2004)

- Outdoor expenditure (including transport): 5.5%
- Radio: 3.1%
- Cinema: 1.0%

*source: Advertising Association's Statistics Yearbook 2006

The marketing communication plan—key elements

Situational awareness entails consideration of factors like current sales, market share, the age of the existing product or service range, and the nature of the competition. A useful tool here is SWOT analysis, referred to on pages 37 & 38. Key objectives may include increasing brand awareness, increasing market share and/or increasing customer retention. Although the general nature and importance of objectives is mentioned on pages 38 & 39 (goal-setting), in the context of

Figure 58: Elements of a marketing plan.

marketing communication, emphasis must be placed on both marketing and communication objectives. Comments at the top of page 39 indicate the type of objective-setting orientation that is required, but objectives need to be specific and realistic: 'increase market share by 6% over the next financial year'; 'increase product availability throughout all outlets within six months', are examples in this respect.

Marketing communication objectives cover a whole range of marketing-supporting activities. Examples can include:

- To re-establish the Z Phone as the must-have accessory for the 16–34 age group
- To increase customer retention by 15% within eighteen months
- To reposition the Thirst-Quencher as the health drink for upwardly mobile men and women

A marketing communications strategy is like other business strategies in many respects. Firstly, it indicates the general direction that the particular aspect of the business is heading. Secondly, it summarises the various tactics employed to achieve the desired outcome. And thirdly, it integrates all the different elements of the process in question. Where marketing communication is concerned, prime elements include decisions regarding target markets, the selection of the communication methods to be used, and the sequence of their use.

Important questions need to be asked at this stage, like:

- Why are we conducting a marketing campaign?

- Who is the target group?
- How does the product/service sit in the current market (positioning)?
- What are the key messages?
- What is the best media vehicle(s)?

Extract from a sample marketing communication plan for VitaDrinks UK plc

Current situation	The company's flagship product, VitaDrink, is currently marketed as a tonic to aid recovery from illness; it has a 21% share of the market. Its customer base lies mainly with young children and the elderly. Recent customer research indicates that the drink has also become popular with young mothers. Though the company has contracts with private and public healthcare providers, it is mainly sold through pharmacists and other retail outlets such as supermarkets	
Key objectives	There are two main objectives: firstly, to consolidate the current customer base for VitaDrink, and extend it to young mothers. The second objective is to create and aggressively market a new drink, 'VitaGen'. The target market will be the highly lucrative, health-conscious 18–30 group	
Strategy	**VitaDrink**	**VitaGen**
	Create a new advertisement campaign with emphasis on VitaDrink as the *family* remedy to aid recovery from illness	A variety of marketing activities to launch VitaGen as *the* health drink for the health-conscious. Various media to be used
	Re-launch VitaDrink with new TV ad to coincide with winter season (October start). Priority given to daytime TV (ITV1). Support with regional radio ads. Family focus for both TV and radio. Follow-up ads in health-related and women's magazines	A series of TV ads with sports personalities, young professionals and activity-based situations. Appropriate internet sites to be targeted, with relevant lifestyle links Short ads on relevant radio stations
Key messages	– VitaDrink, the all family tonic that aids recovery from cold, flu and other ailments – Contains essential vitamins necessary for rejuvenating the system after illness	– VitaGen, the latest health-promoting and energy-boosting drink – Used by leading athletes and sports people
Key messages	– Recommended by pharmacists, leading doctors and health care providers	– Essential for maintaining top performance at work and at leisure – Available as a still or carbonated product in a variety of flavours

(*continued on next page*)

(*continued*)

Promotional activities	– In-store activities (e.g., taster sessions) – Discount coupons in relevant magazines – Predominant displays in national pharmacy chains and supermarkets	– Poster campaign in health studios and fitness clubs – Dispensing machines in prime locations (discount for consumer—first six months) – Free samples at sporting and leisure occasions
Monitoring/evaluation	– Has the re-launch of VitaDrink resulted in increased sales? – What has been the reaction to the various promotional activities for both brands? – What is the weekly feedback on sales and other data for both brands? – What is the weekly feedback on promotional activities for both brands? – Does anything need fine-tuning? (re-orientate strategy/detailed action plan)	

Other examples of detailed tactics are given on page 84

Marketing Communications checklist for VitaDrink and VitaGen ✓

- Do both brands have a clear and consistent image? (e.g., on TV, in print, online and in person)
- Can information about the brands be readily accessed? (e.g., in-store and company website)
- Does consumer research confirm a clear and consistent marketing message for both products
- What has proved the most effective vehicle across the various media (both brands)?
- Can consumers differentiate between VitaDrink and VitaGen (product differentiation)?
- How good is the product information in retail sites?
- Are we getting buy-in from the target groups (to what extent)?
- How good is our customer service/product support?

8.4 Advertising

Whilst advertising vehicles like TV commercials continue to be creative and interesting, the traditional approach to advertising is going through significant change. This change has occurred for a number of reasons: consumers have become more media savvy (the impact of traditional messages is diluted); the growth and sophistication of media-related technology has opened up new opportunities (e.g., the internet, websites, 3G phones); and the move towards the integrated approach to marketing communications mentioned previously. This situation is compounded by the fact that consumers now live in an information age and, consequently, demand more information about products and services than traditional advertising media allow for. All of this means that contemporary marketing messages need to be disseminated and supported by a broad range of marketing communication tools.

Despite the situation outlined above, advertising meets certain elements of the communication needs more effectively than others. It accomplishes this in three main ways:

Process	**Concept**
– by disseminating information about a product or service	**Informational**
– by changing attitudes in a way that is beneficial to the product or service	**Attitudinal**
– by encouraging the consumer to buy the product or service	**Motivational**

Advertising is particularly effective when consumer awareness about the product is low; when a new product or service is about to be launched; the product has unique selling points or features that are not immediately apparent; or there is a need for product differentiation. The success of a particular advertisement campaign is judged by the extent to which it moves the consumer along the continuum from product knowledge and increased awareness, to product purchase.

Just as in IMC in general, advertisers differ in their approaches; one such difference is the push or pull strategy. A *push* strategy is designed to push the particular product hard into distribution channels. Key to success here is a well-trained sales force supported by relevant promotions. On the other hand, a *pull* strategy is aimed at pulling customers into the store or distribution channels, and getting them to pull the product off the shelf. Again, an important element for the pull strategy is investment in advertisement to create demand.

Because of the many variables involved in the decision to buy, it is impossible to accurately state how advertising actually works. It is for this reason that market communicators adopt an objective led approach. This places focus on three main areas: what the communicator is trying to achieve, the best methods for achieving the objectives and the process for measuring success. As with all aspects of the business process, advertising calls for important decisions to be made about key issues: the particular budget, the best media vehicle in the circumstances, content issues and presentation, and how the advertisement process will be monitored and evaluated.

Adopting an objective led approach for advertising also facilitates a strategic approach; this, in turn, complements the overall strategic aim of the marketing communications process. However, it is important to remember that a crucial difference between an advertising objective and a marketing objective, in the wider context, is that an advertising objective can only be achieved by the advertising element of the marketing communication mix.

Many of the processes that apply to marketing communications in general, also apply to advertising:

- The examination of trends (e.g., current sales, market share and the overall trend of the market)
- What is the brand positioning (how do customers perceive the brand)?
- Gaining competitor intelligence
- Existing and potential customer profiles
- Product analysis (e.g., unique selling points; how does it compare with the products of competitors?)

Research & Analysis

Advertising Campaign Strategy

Message Development

Detailed Planning

**Media Plan
(Media Vehicle Selection)**

Figure 59: Stages in the advertising process.

Following the above steps enables the advertising professional to identify key objectives and the overall strategy to be adopted. Indeed, the research process itself reflects the various elements of the strategy: product positioning, product benefits, target group(s) and the related objectives.

The practical process of advertising development starts with the creative brief (this is the outcome of the research and analysis procedure mentioned above). Armed with the important information of the brief, the account director and the creative team can now develop the vital advertising concepts and messages. Once client approval has been given, the further stages of production, piloting (if time permits) and roll-out can be pursued.

Key considerations for the business advertiser

Is advertising appropriate?	e.g., direct mail linked to a clearly defined target market, or public relations?
Setting clear goals	e.g., brand awareness, new product launch, changing customer attitudes
Identifying the target group	e.g., age group (housewives, young professionals)
Selecting the key message	e.g., product benefits
What reaction?	e.g., increase market share
What medium/vehicle?	e.g., TV, radio, newspapers, internet (CPT is a vital factor)

Monitoring effectiveness   e.g., calculate total cost of campaign against number of new sales (cost of each new sale)

Using an agency   e.g., if costs are around the £10,000 range (have they experience in the medium?)

8.5 Sales promotion

In a way, all marketing is a form of promotion, since the objective is to promote the product, brand or the business organisation itself. However, the term 'sales promotion' is usually held to refer to all forms of non-media marketing communication. Examples here are price promotions, exhibitions and sponsorship activities. Sales promotions are essentially short-term incentives aimed at consumers and the trade. These have grown in popularity in recent years, and the reasons for this are: cost effectiveness; the growth of relationship marketing; higher consumer expectations; and retailers requiring product support. Fears that sales promotions can actually damage a brand (e.g., price discounting) are one of the reasons why the life of promotions is usually a short one (usually a few weeks).

The scope of sales promotions normally includes customer promotions (e.g., free samples and gifts) and trade promotions (e.g., discounts). The actual form that the promotion takes ranges from point of sales materials and packaging to direct mail (e.g., competitions). Sales promotions have disadvantages as well as advantages, and some of these are shown in figure 60.

Whereas advertising triggers the early stages of the buying process (like awareness-raising), sales promotions tend to activate latter stages such as purchasing or increased usage. One reason for this is that sales promotions are action oriented. Nevertheless, the demand for quick results through the use of sales promotions can result in consumers thinking that the only competitive advantage is price. Moreover, as credit card providers have found, special promotions (e.g., zero interest on transfers) can simply result in a fickle customer base; many customers tend to move when the interest free period is over.

Sales Promotions

Advantages	Disadvantages
Cost Effective	Short-term effect
Easy-to-measure response	Can obscure brand image
Quick achievement of objectives	Brand can be damaged

Figure 60:

One way of avoiding some of the disadvantages associated with sales promotions is to ensure a careful match between the specific promotional objective and the promotional tool selected. For instance, if the objective is to increase the usage of the product, then this should be matched with a price reduction for multiple packs or orders. Yet another strategy to increase usage would be to devise a gift or competition that needs a minimum number of coupons. As with other aspects of IMC, the success of sales promotions lies in careful research, clearly defined objectives, a strategy that meets long-term marketing and communication objectives, and the perceptive choice of an outside agency, if required.

8.6 Direct mail (DM)

DM has already been briefly referred to and is, of course, the use of postal services to distribute promotional material to target groups. DM is particularly suitable for products that have strong selling points.

Improvements in technology and the quality of DM also allows for better targeting, increased flexibility and greater personalisation. The nature of the DM process means that orders tend to be achieved more quickly. In addition, it is more cost effective since there is no 'middleman'. Where businesses are concerned, DM has many uses, from market research and product launches, to follow up activities and the generation of sales leads.

Whilst all forms of marketing communication are optimised by an integrated approach, the inclusion of DM in the integration process has been found to be particularly beneficial. For example, although a TV campaign can raise product and brand awareness on a broad front, the additional use of DM can maximise the campaign effort through the targeting of key groups.

Despite all of the above positive features of DM, it does suffer an image problem, and is often referred to as 'junk mail'; moreover, initial set up costs can be quite high (e.g., a database). However, potential problems such as these can be mitigated by seeing DM as a long-term proposition (e.g., repeat business), and better identification of the target group can help lessen the junk aspect.

8.7 Telemarketing (TM)

Yet another form of marketing activity is TM. By its very nature, it is more interactive than DM, and takes the form of incoming and outgoing calls at free or special rates. Outgoing TM involves the consumer phoning dedicated numbers for free, or at special rates. Technology has enabled large numbers of calls to be made to consumers (incoming TM) during one operation. However, this same technology has caused particular problems in the UK, because many consumers have received 'ghost' or silent calls. In addition, large numbers of consumers are irritated by receiving calls at inconvenient times.

As the section on IMC has revealed, the marketing communication mix is comprised of elements such as traditional advertising media, non-media communications tools and even personal selling. Understanding buyer behaviour is crucial to the whole marketing communication process, and consequently, information about the product or service (and how this is communicated) is of paramount importance.

Summary

- The introduction of marketing to the business process brought the important element of planning to the whole practice of identifying, anticipating and meeting customer requirements

- Integrated marketing communication is a concept or strategy that combines all aspects of marketing communication such as advertising, sales, promotion, public relations and direct response
- Understanding the target market and buyer behaviour is fundamental to developing a market communication strategy
- Key elements that impact marketing communication are beliefs, attitudes, standards and intentions
- Marketing communication success depends upon knowledge relating to: information about what motivates buyers; information on incomes and lifestyles; an intrinsic understanding of a product's unique selling points
- A key tenet of media planning is maximum coverage at minimum cost
- Whether the media vehicle is television, newspapers, magazines or other mediums, key factors regarding cost are: prominence (where it appears), regularity (how often it appears), and duration (how long the campaign is)
- A marketing communication plan has vital elements like situational awareness, key objectives, overall strategy and a detailed action plan
- Advertising is an important media vehicle and aids marketing communications by disseminating information about the product or service, changing attitudes in a way that is beneficial to the product or service, and encouraging the consumer to buy the product or service

Tutorial

1. a. Select three leading brands in the same product area, and conduct a survey with a view to discovering why consumers prefer one brand over another
   b. Analyse the results of the above survey and determine what the responses reveal about the effectiveness of each product's marketing campaign
2. Using the information given in this chapter:
   a. Decide how you might improve upon an existing product's marketing communication strategy

   or

   b. Devise a completely new marketing communication plan for a product or service of your choice
3. Collect a number of different newspapers and magazines, and review the advertisements within them. Evaluate how the 'messages' differ in terms of product selling points and the targeting of social groups, income levels, gender and lifestyles

9 Protecting the business— crisis management

One-minute overview

The risk of a crisis is part of the business-operating environment. Whereas in the past, only companies operating in high-risk sectors such as gas, oil and airlines tended to have a crisis management plan, now even those in the toy business have them. As the case studies in this chapter confirm, business crises that are badly handled can do significant damage to the brand image, and the organisation as a whole

This chapter will enable you to:

- Recognise that business crises can take different forms
- Understand that crises can go through certain stages
- Appreciate how important it is for companies to react to crises quickly, openly and honestly
- Grasp how critical it is to have a crisis management plan
- Be aware of the necessity to have a crisis communication plan
- Realise the importance of engaging positively with the media
- Understand the steps to be taken when instituting a product recall

9.1 The nature of a business crisis

No matter what type of business you operate, or where you are in the market place, there will always be inherent risks; it is simply part of the operational environment. The crisis environment is markedly different from the usual stress of the day-to-day business environment. The intense stress of the crisis situation can lead to distorted perceptions (e.g., seeing issues as mutually exclusive—the company or the consumer?), flawed decisions (or no decisions at all), failure to communicate and a feeling of powerlessness and loss of control.

Business crises tend to have common characteristics: they nearly always take the form of bad news; they can undermine the reputation and credibility of the organisation; and they can cause significant disruption to the running of the organisation.

A business crisis can be seen to go through certain stages:

1. Complete surprise (e.g., the media knew about the Tylenol problem before J&J—see following case studies)
2. There is a lack of quality information about the issue (what *exactly* has gone wrong?)
3. Senior management have a feeling the crisis is taking a life of its own (the media again)

4. There is a clear choice to be made regarding the response to the crisis
5. If the right choice has been made (the correct response), management starts to regain the situation

The spate of floods in the UK during 2007 demonstrated that not only business organisations were decimated, but whole communities. Even a 'simple' fire, and the efforts to contain it, can do untold damage to key business data and equipment. Other potential threats to businesses and company reputations include: flawed or contaminated products, legal action, industrial disputes, a major interruption in production or services, system failures, or an issue surrounding a senior executive. One only has to look at an example of the last category to see the damage that can be caused to the organisation by one individual. In this case, by senior executives making unfortunate comments:

The PR gaffes of senior executives

Despite the fact that executives should know better, examples abound of some of them demonstrating a supreme lack of judgement. They can do tremendous damage by making comments that are construed by others as a criticism of how the business operates, its products, services, suppliers or customers.

In the UK, the phrase 'Doing a Ratner', describes such an executive faux pas. 'Doing a Ratner' has its origins in the occasion when Gerald Ratner (of the Ratner jewellery chain) made the following comments during a speech to the Institute of Directors in April 1991:

"We also do cut-glass sherry decanters complete with six glasses on a silver-plated tray that your butler can serve you drinks on, all for £4.95. People say, 'How can you sell this for a low price'? **I say, because it's total crap***" (writer's emphasis)*

Unfortunately, Ratner made matters worse by going on to remark that some of the company's earrings were *"cheaper than a M&S prawn sandwich but probably wouldn't last as long"*. Although Ratner maintained that his remarks were made at a private function, were not to be taken seriously, and that he did not expect them to be reported—the damage was done.

Some £500 million pounds was wiped from the value of the company. Ratner later left the company, and the brand, irrevocably damaged, became the Signet Group. This matter also serves to confirm what has already been stated—rarely is anything off the record.

In March 1998, Freddy Shepherd and Douglas Hall (bosses of Newcastle United football club) were the subject of a newspaper expose that alleged they called Geordie (i.e., Newcastle-born) women 'dogs'. In addition, it was alleged that **the two men mocked fans for purchasing £50 replica football shirts that cost the club £5.**

In July 2000, David Shepherd, brand director of the clothing chain 'Topman', stated in a trade publication that his customers were hooligans, and went on to comment, *"Very few of our customers have to wear suits to work.* **They'll be for his first interview or first court case".**

In October 2003, Mike Barrett, the chief executive of British bank Barclays, stated to a parliamentary Treasury committee, on credit cards: *"I don't borrow on credit cards. I have four children.* **I give them advice not to pile up debts on their credit cards".**

More recently, in September 2007, Tony Hayward (the new boss of British Petroleum) stated that the current performance of the company was 'dreadful'—**almost £4 billion was wiped off its share value.**

Notwithstanding unfortunate comments or behaviour of senior executives, events external to the organisation can have a potentially catastrophic impact on it. How the organisation responds to the developing crisis, especially in the first few hours, can make the difference between weathering the storm (and regaining threatened reputations and market share), or going under.

9.2 Corporate case studies—Johnson and Johnson

The Tylenol crisis in 1982, involving American pharmaceutical giant Johnson and Johnson (J&J) is a case in point. J&J's global sales, across thousands of diverse products, amounted to £24.6 billion ($47 billion). Since its flotation on the stock exchange in 1944, J&J established a reputation as a socially responsible organisation (e.g., it donated more than $80 million worth of healthcare products to help victims of the Asian tsunami disaster). J&J's whole business philosophy was expressed in its 'credo':

> *"We believe our first responsibility is to doctors, nurses, and patients, to mothers and fathers and all others who use our products and services"*

J&J's credo, and the manner in which its CEO implemented it, was to save it from one of the potentially worst corporate disasters of the decade.

Before the crisis, Tylenol was the most successful, over-the-counter product in the US, with over one million users. It was the leader in the painkiller field, with 37% of the market share. The painkiller was responsible for 19% of J&J's corporate profits for the first three quarters of 1982, and 33% of J&J's year-to-year profit growth. Then, in the autumn of 1982, a person or persons unknown deliberately contaminated Tylenol capsules with cyanide and placed the tampered-with product on the shelves of pharmacies in the Chicago area; seven people died. The first J&J knew about the tragedy was a phone call from a journalist asking why their trusted product was killing people—the crisis had begun.

Immediately, J&J chairman James Burke formed an executive crisis team, and worked on a priority basis. The first priority was protecting their customers, the second was to save the product. Protecting its customer meant that J&J recalled every Tylenol capsule nationwide. The product recall alone cost $100 million dollars. This action was consolidated by a termination of all advertising for the product.

The swift response to the crisis by J&J was characterised by other actions that became synonymous with good crisis management, they:

- Communicated immediately with the media
- Used the media to communicate with the public
- Established a customer hotline
- Established a hotline for daily media updates
- Co-operated closely with regulatory authorities

Although the advertising campaign ran by J&J during its immediate response was aimed at reassuring the public, there was some criticism of the sales-pitch slant adopted.

A key reason for this was that J&J was a conservative organisation, and therefore its in-house media team were more experienced in advertising and marketing rather than PR. However, as already indicated, once this was realised, all product advertising ceased.

As mentioned above, the thread running through the whole issue of crisis management was public safety. This concern was reinforced by the appearance of the CEO on popular TV current affair shows and major press conferences held at corporate headquarters. The overall message to the general public was one of action to address the issue (product recall); that their concerns were being taken seriously (the hotlines and consumer feedback strategies); and, above all, that the company had nothing to hide (information, information, information). All of this was cemented by the close working relationship between J&J's in-house media team and the external PR agency.

Equally important as the initial strategy for coping with the crisis, is the *comeback plan*. In the case of J&J, this was made easier by their genuine concern for public safety. Telling the public *not* to purchase their product, the immediate and extensive product recall, and the constant information campaign, not only reassured the public, but also reinforced the view that here was a genuine and honest company that had become the victim of a vicious poisoner.

In addition to J&J's public concern being the bedrock of its comeback, they adopted the following strategies:

- The positive and effective 'socially responsible' PR campaign continued
- A press conference at company headquarters
- A new marketing campaign was launched
- Tylenol were now contained in a tamper-resistant pack (the first of its kind)
- Discounts were offered (e.g., up to 25%)
- Sales teams gave thousands of presentations up and down the country to medical professionals

As the previous case studies reveal, when a crisis occurs, organisations have two clear choices: either to be proactive and communicate openly, or adopt a bunker mentally and wait as the media lay siege. If the latter choice is made, the organisation will be continually on the defensive as piece-by-piece, more and more damaging information about the crisis is revealed. As the Cadbury situation confirms (see below), such a stance also leaves the organisation very vulnerable to legal action by regulatory authorities and consumers. At least one legal action against J&J was dismissed by the judge on the grounds that the company had made every effort to notify the public of the dangers associated with the product.

Media and communication academics not only cite J&J's response to their corporate crisis as a model of exemplary practice, but also hold that their strategies conformed to particular theories. Although the following brief examples of such theories are related in some way, or are dimensions of the same theory (e.g., *remediation* and *rectification* are both forgiveness strategies), they have been treated separately to aid understanding.

Suffering theory – Related to 'forgiveness and sympathy' theory, suffering theory relates to how the company sees its position. For example, 'this is not our fault, we are the unwitting victims of … we too are suffering'

Forgiveness & Sympathy – this strategy is designed to solicit understanding and forgiveness from those affected and the general public

Remediation – Some form of compensation is offered to the victims. Although they were not responsible for the product tampering, J&J gave financial help and professional counselling to those affected

Rectification – This entails taking action to ensure that the crisis is unlikely to occur again (J&J's tamper-resistant packaging and new inspection procedures)

The exxon valdez disaster

Unfortunately, some organisations do not learn from the experiences and examples of others, and the Exxon Valdez oil disaster is a case in point. In March 1989, the Exxon Valdez oil tanker ran aground in Alaska's Prince William Sound, spilling 250,000 barrels of oil (equivalent to 10 million gallons). The result was an environmental disaster of monumental proportions; probably the worst man-made environmental disaster to date. Whereas J&J's response to their crisis was regarded as a textbook example of crisis management, the Exxon Corporation's response would be held as a textbook example by many of how to *mismanage* a crisis.

Since the J&J crisis in 1982, organisations hit with a disaster had to be seen to be doing two key things. Firstly, they must be perceived as actively seeking a solution to the problem (*immediately* engaging in crisis management activities). Secondly, the organisation must be seen as creating a positive image of how the crisis is being handled (public and stakeholder perception is everything). In other words, two crucial elements need to be present:

1. A crisis management plan
2. A crisis management *communication* plan

(The above will be dealt with further in this section)

From their point of view, Exxon executives took all the necessary action. For example, they:

- Made themselves available
- Engaged in open communication and answered journalist's questions
- Held regular press conferences (daily during the first ten days of the disaster)
- Provided substantial detail on their Valdez operation

Despite the Exxon's perceptions of their efforts, however, others had a starkly different view:

- Exxon was criticised for refusing to acknowledge the extent of the problem
- Company executives were held not to have commented on the crisis for almost a week
- The CEO was criticised for waiting six days to make a statement, and for not visiting the scene of the disaster for almost three weeks

In addition to the above negative comments, and the claim that cleaning up the oil was their top priority, it took Exxon nearly ten hours to deploy oil-containing booms. Whilst there may have been understandable reasons for some of the responses (e.g., legal advice, and genuine logistical problems), interested parties and the general public were left with the impression that Exxon were not treating the disaster with the seriousness it deserved.

Not only was the communication delayed and held to be more limited than Exxon's perception, the company insisted on communicating from Valdez itself. A small town, with limited communication means, the choice of Valdez as a communications centre simply compounded the perceived negativity of the whole situation.

As if things could not deteriorate further, Exxon took out full-page newspaper advertisements costing nearly $2 million that included an apology for the oil spill. However, the adverts did not clearly accept responsibility for the cause of the disaster. This simply incensed people further, and exacerbated an already fraught situation.

There is no doubt that the scale of the disaster would be overwhelming for any organisation, and Exxon may well have had a sound crisis communication plan. Nevertheless, the severity of the legal judgement points to the fact that, if a coherent plan existed, the priorities made left a lot to be desired. Further, they appeared not to have accurately judged the communication implications as quickly as the situation demanded.

There is no doubt that Exxon made repeated attempts to disseminate information, but it is not just the flow of information or its regularity that matters, but its *quality*. For instance, J&J conducted daily consumer research to determine how the respondents felt about the matter. Even the act of conducting such research, communicates concern on the part of the organisation.

As highlighted earlier in this work, when individuals or organisations refuse to communicate, or comment belatedly, a communication vacuum is created that others (and especially the media) are only too happy to fill. Imagery is a powerful communicator, and whereas for J&J, the image was one of product recall and human loss; and for the UK's Northern Rock Bank (in September 2007), high streets filled with customers queuing to withdraw their money; for Exxon in 1989, the lasting image was one of wildlife dying in rivers of black oil.

Apart from the impact on habitat and wildlife, the overall cost of the Exxon disaster at Prince William Sound was a clean-up bill of $2.5 billion; $1.5 billion in compensation claims; and a Federal court fine of some $5 billion (later appealed). As with many company crises deemed to be handled badly, the ultimate casualty was the reputation of the company. Several years after the disaster, consumer research revealed that nearly 55% of respondents were negatively disposed towards Exxon and its products.

The Cadbury Schweppes salmonella crisis

Yet another, more recent example of a less than satisfactory response to crisis management occurred in the UK during 2006. Cadbury's, a UK leader in the confectionery and food field (especially chocolate), discovered that their products might contain salmonella. Despite the fact that the company had suspicions about the contaminated products between January and March 2006, a product recall was not made until the 23rd of June.

The salmonella product contamination resulted in over forty people falling ill (many were children) and the eventual recall of more than a million bars of chocolate. Commentators and interested parties estimated the cost of the product recall at £5 million, and the loss of sales and correction procedures at some £20 million. On top of this, the court fined Cadbury's nearly £1 million in total. Some commentators estimated the true total cost of the refusal to disclose at £30 million.

For a company of Cadbury's history, affection and standing in the UK, the court charges were particularly damning. Three charges in particular would no doubt dismay those who held the company in high esteem:

1. Selling unsafe chocolate during the period in question
2. Failing to immediately inform the authorities
3. Not operating an effective hazard and detection policy

It beggars belief that, despite the existence or absence of a crisis communication policy, a company of Cadbury's standing would seek to continue selling a product they even suspected of being contaminated with salmonella. In addition, *each* charge carries a penalty of two years in prison, and *unlimited* fines.

As soon as a company even thinks it may have a contamination problem, the following actions need to be taken:

- Stop all production of the suspected products immediately
- Conduct rigorous product, equipment and procedure tests (and risk analysis)
- Inform regulatory bodies immediately of any concerns
- Conduct relevant laboratory tests
- Confirm or clear suspected contamination (confirmed by another lab?)
- If contamination is confirmed, meet all safety, regulatory and public obligations
- Inform senior executives, key stakeholders and other interested parties
- Form a senior executive crisis team
- Execute the crisis *management* plan, and crisis *communication* plan (immediacy, openness, information flow and public concern are the priorities)

Although the recommended actions above take the form of a prioritised list, the situation can be so serious (as in the case of Cadbury's) that executives need to be charged with pursuing specific responsibilities simultaneously. One question should be paramount in any business crisis, and act as a guide for all responses—*what is the right thing to do?*

The northern rock bank crisis

The UK's Northern Rock Bank crisis in September 2007 (referred to earlier), progressively deepened despite almost daily communication from the bank, and government assurances that they would guarantee investor's money. This highlights the fact that, despite how rational the information is (and how good the flow), people may still behave 'irrationally'. A number of factors came into play in the Northern Rock situation that had a significant bearing on how the crisis unfolded:

- People who put their money into savings accounts are normally risk averse
- Any perceived element of risk is intensified when the money is their life savings
- Corporate and other scandals have led to increased distrust of public and business figures in general (no matter how high the integrity of individuals is)

It is difficult to see how Northern Rock could have done things differently once the news broke about their need to borrow funds. It has to be recognised that, even where the crisis has been responded to immediately, openly, honestly, and with the well-being of consumers in mind, an organisation can simply be overtaken by events. If the Northern Rock crisis demonstrates anything, it is that organisations need to treat perceptions as fact, and recognise the power of the media to influence public opinion—this is why it is so crucial to keep the media 'on-side'.

If, despite the best communication efforts of an organisation, the crisis escalates beyond their control, at least the individuals involved can say that they did the right thing. Such a situation is crucial for the reputation of the individuals concerned, the credibility of the particular sector, and any potential legal action.

9.3 Crisis management—principles, procedures and plans

Crises can be seen to fall into certain categories: the *smouldering crisis* (no clear action has been taken by the organisation, and the issue takes a life of its own and gets steadily worse); the *perceptual crisis* (there is no real crisis, but some people think there is); the sudden crisis, (which, as its name indicates, no one in the company is immediately aware of).

A classic example of a perceptual crisis is the situation where a bank does not have a major problem (or no problem at all), but its customers *perceive* there is a problem and withdraw their funds. This, of course, causes the crisis that did not exist in the first place. It is for this reason that organisations cannot afford to ignore any form of crisis, whether real or imagined. The smouldering crisis and the perceptual crisis have a common thread: either the organisation does not have a crisis plan, it is not being implemented properly, or the efforts of the company to meet the crisis are rendered useless by the high degree of consumer concern (e.g., the Northern Rock situation).

Whatever the issue, it is vital to have some sort of planned response. As the previous case studies confirm, how a company communicates during a crisis determines not only how it will be perceived by consumers or others in the market place, but also whether or not the company survives at all. In some cases, companies who communicated well during a crisis actually strengthened their position in eyes of regulators, consumers and the sector as a whole. A key factor in surviving a crisis is the relationship the company has with the media (and the media skills of key personnel).

But good relations with key media players alone is not enough. As has been highlighted before, two crucial elements are also required: the crisis plan itself (how the company will deal with the particular issue), and the crisis communication plan (how the company will communicate with the media and the public during the crisis). One common crisis that faces many companies and tests these two elements is the product recall situation.

Product recalls

A product recall is a public request to return to the supplier or manufacturer, a specific batch or entire run of a product. Whilst the problem may involve quality issues, a key concern is any threat to consumer health or safety. Product recalls are a frequent feature of business life, and statistics relating to the food industry alone highlight this fact. In 2006, across Europe, over 2,885 product recalls were made. Unless serious injury or death results, and the process is handled properly, no lasting damage should occur to the reputation of the individual or the organisation.

In addition to the J&J and Cadbury cases mentioned previously, notable recalls include:

- 1998–1999 (USA) – The Chevrolet Malibu incident. Failure to recall resulted in fatalities
- 2000 (USA) – The Ford Motor Company's recall of 6.5 million Firestone tyres fitted to their Explorer model resulted in the resignation of the then CEO
- 2005 (UK & Canada) – Potentially carcinogenic Sudan 1 was found in over 400 products containing Worcester sauce
- 2006 (various countries) – Dell recalls over 4 million potentially faulty notebook batteries made by Sony. There were some instances where the batteries overheated or caught fire
- 2007 (USA) – Mattel recalls 17.5 million toys
- 2007 (USA) – The US Consumer Product Safety Division withdraws 601,000 toys and children's jewellery over fears that the lead content exceeded safety levels

Businesses should have the following key aims where product recalls are concerned: to minimise the risk of injury or death; to minimise the cost and inconvenience to the consumer; and to minimise the need for compulsory regulatory intervention by complying with the law (but the authorities should always be informed immediately over any product concerns).

Generating key information is one of the crucial steps in the product recall process. Important information should include: a clear description of the product (e.g., make, model, serial or batch number and date of manufacture); details of the threat, hazard or risk; what action the consumer has to take; contact details of the manufacturer/supplier, and how the product is to be returned (e.g., returned to the local supermarket).

Though some companies are reluctant to do so for legal reasons, *an apology goes a long way* in helping to restore consumer confidence.

At the same time, the manufacturer needs to send the above information (and any additional details where required) to wholesalers, suppliers, retailers and export agents etc. Another vital element in the product recall process is the identification and analysis of relevant records; and the monitoring of returns against these. But, above all, the communication of the issue to the general public should have the highest priority.

The methods used to communicate the product recall to the public depend upon the extent of the problem and the perceived impact. Whilst the most used method of communicating with the public is newspaper advertisements, press releases to other media such as radio and television may be necessary. Some countries stipulate the minimum size for product recall and similar ads, and it is often recommended that the ad appears within a certain number of pages (e.g., the first four or five). Whatever the specific national regulations, it is commonsense that the ad appears in a prominent position in the paper. Many organisation also make full use of their website, and trade publications along with publicity material in retail outlets helps maximise the effort.

It is important to stress in any communication, that the cost of the recall will be met by the company. Additional examples of good practice are the creation of free telephone hotlines, and other sources of further information (e.g., company website). The preparation of FAQs related to any concerns that the consumer may have (e.g., physical symptoms if the product is eaten), is another positive step.

The crisis management plan (CMP)

Traditionally, the business organisations that developed crisis management plans were those in 'high risk' sectors like gas, oil and airlines. Now, even toy manufacturers see the necessity to have a CMP. A properly designed CMP will help to: protect the safety of employees and the general public; minimise injury or damage; reduce stress and emotional trauma; minimise the negative impact on the brand image; aid the recovery of the organisation. Whilst CMPs can vary from organisation to organisation, and sector to sector, common elements can be identified:

- The crisis management plan itself
- Administration and execution details
- The crisis management team (CMT)
- The creation of a crisis communication centre (CCC)
- The crisis communication plan

Although organisations cannot plan for all eventualities, a useful starting point is a professionally conducted risk assessment, and written protocols for a variety of potential crises. Other important elements of a CMP include:

- Details of the senior person responsible for leading a crisis-response
- A clear chain of command (and alternative personnel as 'back-ups')
- A 'hierarchy of responses' (e.g., 'safety first')
- The execution of evacuation procedures and associated arrangements
- Procedures and details regarding training

Administration and execution

Natural disasters such as fire, floods and other crises like systems failures are, in a relative sense, easier to plan for than a crisis that directly threatens the reputation of the organisation. Natural disaster planning entails procedures like emergency drills, systems back-up, duplicates of key records (e.g., financial, employee, customers and suppliers), alternate premises and arrangements for equipping these. Above all, training is essential for ensuring that everyone knows the part they need to play, and for generating confidence and expertise.

Good administration is necessary for the execution of an emergency plan. Details should be held centrally of blueprints of the building(s) with associated fire escapes, assembly points etc.; an up-to-date employee list, with details of staff who need assistance with evacuation; names of employees who have received first aid training; and the names of persons in each department who are responsible for co-ordinating crisis events 'locally' ('employee accounting' is a vital factor in coping with any crisis, especially a natural disaster or terrorist incident). Copies of these records must be made, with at least one being stored off-site; all key crisis personnel (and their back-ups) must be aware of their location.

The crisis management team

The CMT is pivotal to the success of the crisis plan and examples of key roles are: team leader and co-ordinator, PR advisor, legal advisor, situation and media monitor, spokesperson, technical advisor. For the CMT to be highly effective, it is important that they engage in some sort of scenario planning. A vital aspect here is role-playing using 'what if' scenarios (e.g., 'What if a fire completely destroyed our premises?' 'What if our new product developed a major fault?' 'What if our main supplier went bankrupt?'). Such realistic training, involving the entire CMT, is essential for developing key skills, generating alternative plans, and focusing minds on the premise that a major crisis is a distinct possibility in the modern business environment.

The crisis communication centre

The creation of a properly resourced crisis communication centre (CCC) is another vital element of the crisis management plan. The previous case studies emphasised how important it is to have an accessible (from the media point of view) and properly resourced CCC. Essential equipment includes: TVs, radios, computers with internet facilities, faxes, multiple phone lines, lists of key contacts (e.g., media figures, stakeholders, regulatory authorities and consumer organisations, etc.). Thought must also be given to back-up systems as well as alternate sources of power such a generators.

Consideration must also be given as to whether to hold press briefings, press conferences and media interviews on company premises (accessibility, 'we have nothing to hide'). In such circumstances, the immediacy of the CCC would be a significant asset. However, this has to be weighed against the possibility that the presence of the media may add to employee stress during the crisis. Another matter for consideration is whether to have a joint CCC with other agencies (e.g., the emergency services), since this might give a greater degree of control as to what key messages are being communicated.

9.4 The crisis communication plan

The crisis communication plan (CCP) is perhaps the most important element of the crisis management process. This because, in an *internal* sense, crisis planning and execution will be undermined if key personnel do not know what to communicate, to whom to communicate, and when to communicate. In addition, during a crisis, communication in various forms (and alternative means in an emergency) is crucial to ensure that procedures such as evacuations are carried out proficiently.

In an *external* sense, how the crisis is presented to the media and the public will determine, to a large extent, whether the organisation will weather the storm. Again, the case studies considered previously confirm that the key messages, and the manner in which they are presented, are paramount here.

The CCP should not be separate from, but be an integral part of, the organisation's general communication plan (as mentioned previously, this should be the result of an organisational communication audit). Whilst, like all plans, the CCP needs to be flexible, key aspects should include: what is to be communicated (key messages), to whom (key audiences), by what means (the correct medium), with what effect (determined by the specific crisis).

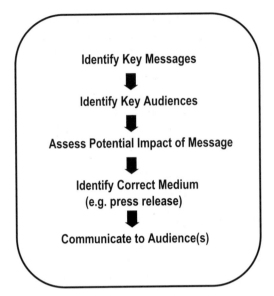

Figure 61: The key message process.

An important factor in determining the communication strategy in a crisis are the answers to questions like: has the cause of the crisis been identified; what has been the impact (e.g., health and safety issues); who has it affected (to what extent?); and are we legally responsible?

It is also prudent to consider the following:

- Who knows at this point? (e.g., the media)
- What might be the short and long-term ramifications?
- Do we have the in-house PR skills to deal with the problem?
- Do we need to execute a product recall (if relevant)?

An organisation's communication response to a crisis must be based on the following premise: 'Tell the whole truth, tell it at once, and tell it quickly'. In other words, get *all* the facts, tell your story first, tell it well, and stay 'on message'. Remember, the first twenty-four hours of any crisis mean the difference between being seen as in control, concerned for others and pursuing a solution; or, being on the 'on the back foot', and under siege.

The member of the crisis management team who has been designated as media co-ordinator and spokesperson must be credible, capable and, preferably, trained. All dealings with the media, and all communication concerning the crisis must be channelled through the spokesperson.

The whole idea behind a CCP is that all the responses to the crisis are planned and co-ordinated, the appropriate communication medium is chosen and the intended impact is carefully considered. Whilst it is useful to have pre-prepared examples of items such as press releases across a range of potential crises, care must be taken that these do not appear as cynical attempts to manipulate key audiences (avoid clichés *at all costs*—see how easy it is to fall into the cliché trap).

Although it is not possible to determine exactly what form particular messages will take, it is possible to address the concerns and expectations of the various audiences in a general way. Most audiences will want information along the following lines:

Cause – a clear account of what went wrong
Explanation – a clear account of why it went wrong
Response – what you are doing about the crisis now
Corrective – how you will prevent it happening in the future
Action

Another useful procedure is to keep a media log. This is a simple record of who said what to whom, along with copies of clippings and recordings (with corresponding dates). Procedures like this are essential for correcting untruths and misrepresentation before they become 'fact'.

As indicated before, it is not unusual for the situation to be confused during the early hours of a crisis, and quality information may not be immediately available. Accordingly, it may not be possible to issue a definitive press release; one way forward is to issue a 'holding statement'. The holding statement is a simple statement of facts as they are known at the time. The construction of the statement needs to be flexible, and allow for greater clarification as more facts emerge. Even in such constrained circumstances, it is still possible to be positive, *"It is too early to say what caused the building to collapse, but the emergency services are working round the clock to rescue those employees who are stilled trapped"*. Under no circumstances should a holding statement contain figures, estimates or any degree of speculation.

Aspects of post crisis recovery have already been alluded to in terms of restoring the reputation of the company and the brand image, but equally important is some form of evaluation as to the effectiveness of the CCP.

Among the essential questions that need to be asked are:

- What about the timings of our responses?
- What about the accuracy of our responses?
- What about the quality of our responses?
- Did we convey the key messages effectively? (e.g., did we address the main audience concerns?)
- Did we develop a good rapport with the media?
- In what ways was our image affected?
- Will any aspect of the negative impact be long-term?
- What communication lessons have we learned?

After the crisis, debrief, document learning points, and amend CCP accordingly.

Crisis management – media checklist ✓

- Be proactive (engage with them)
- Check all information before it is released
- Return all press calls promptly
- Keep a media log (who said what to whom, and when)
- Stay 'on message' (do not deviate from your position unless there is good cause to do so)

- Choose the appropriate medium carefully (e.g., press release? press conference?)
- If you are stuck on a general question, make a specific point; if you are stuck on a specific question, make a general response
- Never say 'no comment'
- Do not get into an argument—you will lose

Summary

- Business crises can be seen to fall into categories such as the smouldering crisis, the perceptual crisis and the sudden crisis
- The intense stress of the business crisis can lead to distorted perceptions, flawed decisions, failure to communicate and a feeling of powerlessness and loss of control
- A successful response to a business crisis entails a strategic response, and the key elements are:
  - the crisis management plan itself
  - the administration and execution of the plan
  - the crisis communication plan
  - the crisis management team
  - the creation of a crisis communication centre
- The Tylenol crisis that hit Johnson and Johnson proved how important it is to:
  - put safety before brand image and the company
  - inform the public and regulatory authorities immediately
  - have a crisis management plan
  - communicate openly, honestly and regularly
  - work positively with the media
- In a business crisis situation, most audiences want information along the lines of: a clear account of what went wrong; an explanation of why it went wrong; what the company is doing to address the situation; and what steps will be taken to prevent a recurrence
- Issues such as product recalls are common features of business life, but how they are executed is crucial for brand image and the reputation of the company
- A post-crisis review is crucial for learning lessons and strengthening the organisation's response should another crisis occur

Tutorial

The following exercises will depend upon the size of the business organisation in question. Accordingly, if a large organisation is concerned, then focus on one particular area.

1. Using an organisation to which you have access, conduct an organisational analysis and:
   a. identify any significant internal issues that could create a potential crisis
   b. identify any external factors that may, along with internal factors, leave the company open to a crisis (or an event that would have a serious detrimental impact on the company)
2. Carry out a communications audit (review pages 24 & 25) and determine if the company is capable of coping with a crisis using the existing communication system
3. a. Examine the company's communication plan and decide whether or not it could be used to respond effectively to a crisis situation
   b. If the communication plan is held to be deficient in some way, correct the deficiencies (if no communication plan exists, use the relevant details in this chapter to create one)
4. Draft sample press releases for the following situations:
   a. A product recall
   b. Customer confidential details have been compromised (e.g., a computer hacker)
   c. A serious systems failure that has inconvenienced hundreds of customers

One-minute overview

The staggering value of business conducted on the internet is evidence that e-commerce is not only here to stay, but will grow at a phenomenal rate. In order to achieve, maintain and develop e-commerce success, businesses need to realise that information and communication are crucial. Within this context, the criticality of the website, customer databases, customer service, the unique nature of online marketing, and the value of email and blogging need to be realised

This chapter will enable you to:

- Recognise the value of e-commerce
- Understand the importance of the business website
- Realise the significance of customer databases
- Be aware of the necessity for high security
- Perceive the value of online marketing, and how it differs from traditional marketing
- Optimise the significance of email and blogging as key tools
- Appreciate the need for proper e-commerce policies and procedures

10.1 E-commerce

"Communications is at the heart of e-commerce and community"

Meg Whitman, ebay Chief Executive

The incredible value of internet business and the crucial role that communication plays in this context is indicated by the immense sums associated with internet business transactions. In 2007, ebay paid £1.4 billion for the internet telephone company Skype. Skype has some 53 million registered users, and states that 2 million people are using its software at any given moment.

More recently, Yahoo is said to have made a £527 million offer for social networking website, Facebook. Founded in 2004, Facebook allows users to post profiles of themselves, and is particularly popular amongst students. Facebook has grown steadily in popularity, and has user numbers estimated at 7.5 million in the US alone. Importantly, Facebook has recently signed an advertising deal with Microsoft. A similar site, Myspace, was bought by the Murdoch News Corporation for $580 million in 2006.

Another indication of the communication and business impact of the internet in the UK was the meteoric success of the pop band, Artic Monkeys. Eschewing traditional music marketing methods, and using a strategy of providing free downloads (supported by live appearances in their native Yorkshire), the Artic Monkeys stormed the charts and took the number one spot twice. But what about ordinary business transactions in the UK and elsewhere, do they justify the significant hype that often surrounds internet business transactions (e-commerce)? The answer is yes, and the following figures are evidence in this respect:

- With online sales of £6.7 billion in 2006, the UK has become Europe's biggest online market. The rise in online sales is attributed to the more extensive use of broadband services and lower costs in this regard. Research organisation Mintel expects total internet sales to triple by 2010
- According to Retail Decisions, a payment processing company, UK online shoppers spent some £700,000 *in sixty seconds* on December 10th, 2007. The Interactive Media Group revealed that over Christmas 2007, UK online shoppers spent £84 million (this was almost treble the 2006 amount)
- US business researchers estimate that total internet sales passed the $100 billion mark in 2007. This figure does not include services such as travel, and is an increase of 24% on US internet sales in 2005
- It is further estimated that in five years time, internet sales will reach 4.7% of total US retails sales (the current internet sales figure stands at 2.7%)

E-commerce is based on the principle of doing business in a way that is more efficient and more cost effective. Although there are initial set-up costs and investment as in any business, entry to the world of online business is quite low compared to conventional start-ups.

E-commerce is the paperless exchange of business information using EDI (electronic data interchange). In the world of e-commerce, information and communication are the keys to success.

The business website

Figure 62 represents the key elements of the online business. The 'shop front' of the online business is the website. Research shows that on average, the website has about eight seconds to grab the attention of the user. This means not only must the site be visually attractive, but it must communicate key information to the potential buyer. Research also confirms that the following information is crucial to potential buyers:

Figure 62: Key elements of the online business.

- Detailed information about the product
- Detailed information about the seller
- Price comparisons
- Information about the security of the transaction

A well designed website should: provide high visibility for all products and services; convert potential customers to actual customers; establish and reinforce the brand image; contain mechanisms for generating repeat business and a customer database. Important aspects here are the use of colour, graphics, the amount of text and where it is placed. How information is used is vital, and clear messages must be sent regarding what your business is, the products and services it offers, and how to navigate the site.

A memorable logo is invaluable for consolidating all the various aspects. These important features of branding must be consistent over all the pages of the site, and the products and services showcased in them. Where websites are concerned, you only have seconds to communicate your competitive advantage and convert prospects to sales.

Great care needs to be taken when considering the domain name for the website, since the domain name is, in many respects, the business. Domain names are considered so important, that some individuals have made fortunes just by anticipating domain names that companies may use, registering these, and then selling them to the companies in question. A sound business communication strategy is to develop multiple, related domain names (figure 63 is an example). These will be related to the primary domain name and can be used to drive additional business.

Choosing a reputable and reliable hosting provider (Internet Service Provider) is as important as the design of the website itself, and a number of issues need to be considered: the nature and extent of service levels; the total storage available; the number of email accounts provided and the important aspect of site security. The ISP itself may offer a secure electronic payment system, or recommend another company that offers the special merchant accounts necessary for accepting payment over the net.

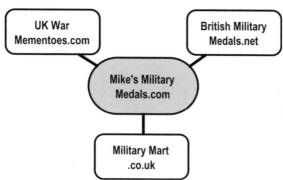

Figure 63: Multiple domain names generate more business.

Once the site is designed and hosted, promotion becomes a crucial business activity. The technical name given to this process is 'search engine optimisation' (SEO); the objective is to rank as high as possible in the maximum number of search engines. This entails identifying and emphasising the key words and phrases associated with the product or service, and all the various pages and tags linked to the site.

The best way of designing any business website is to imagine that you are a potential customer, and ask the following questions:

- Now that I have found the site, what will make me stay and purchase?
- Is all the information well structured and are all the instructions clear?
- Is the site easy to navigate?
- Is the catalogue and 'virtual shop' well organised?
- Are the payment details and instructions clear and easy to follow?
- Do I feel that my financial details are held securely?
- What will make me shop with them again?

Getting feedback on your site is very important, and there are two main ways of doing this: providing a customer feedback mechanism (e.g., 'let us know how we could improve this site and enter our monthly free gift draw'), and using web analysis tools. Although a web analytics package is yet another piece of technology to cope with, it is well worth the investment in time and money. Web analysis produces information on issues such as: how many customers have visited your site (click rate); what are the most popular areas of your site (click density); how the customer arrived at your site (what URLs did they use?); how long the customer stayed at your site overall; the degree of 'bounce rate' (the number of people who stayed at your site for ten seconds or less). All of this information is not just important for improving the website, but also for optimising sales.

Customer databases

The value of a customer database, where e-commerce is concerned, cannot be over-estimated. Whilst intelligence gathering about potential customers is an important part of the database process, existing customer details can provide crucial data. Sources such as purchase details, emails, faxes, invoices, letters and existing customer lists can generate valuable information:

- Contact information   (how can we optimise this?)
- Purchase history   (what are the key products/services?)
- Service history   (e.g., have warranty claims been made, have they product insurance?)
- Account history   (e.g., do they pay on time?)
- Individual details   (e.g., age, gender, income etc.)

Information such as the above allows businesses to profile customers and maximise the impact of marketing campaigns and product development. Vital information is also gained about buying behaviour and customer loyalty. Once compiled, the information is, in fact, the basis of a customer management system (CMS), and decisions need to be made about how the system will be administered. For example, will the system be integrated with other business processes? Will a simple 'DIY' or 'off the shelf' system be used, or will the process be outsourced?

If the CMS process is outsourced, specialist providers can either design a bespoke software package and run the whole process (this can be quite costly), or the business can lease a software package and expertise from the ASP (application service provider). The benefits of working with an ASP is that they can supply services such as 'data mining'. This process entails the analysis and cross-referencing of information patterns and relationships within a database. Data analysis enables the business to identify important trends, and thus better target certain customer groups with the benefits shown in figure 64. This process also allows

Figure 64: The benefits of data analysis.

for more effective use of communication systems such as email. As with many business aspects, cost is a key issue when choosing the CMS solution, and it is important to get a full breakdown of the costs and services offered from the ASP.

Security issues

Whether e-commerce is the core business of a company or simply one aspect of how the organisation markets or sells its products or services, the largely unregulated nature of e-commerce presents a number of security threats. Examples in this respect are:

- Gaining access to customers' personal or financial information
- Attacking the website with a virus
- Cloning a website
- Attempts at fraud
- Forcing a reduction of service, or complete shutdown
- Click fraud
- Gaining access to vital data about the business (e.g., marketing plans, new products, price lists, discounts)

Click fraud has become a significant issue for e-commerce, and occurs when a visitor clicks on an advert with the intent of the payer being charged for the advert. It has been known for some website owners to repeatedly click on their competitor's website adverts to increase costs and thus lower profits. Click fraud can be combated by monitoring and logging server activity (e.g., sudden increases in advert expenditure and clicks from unusual IP addresses), and removing any adverts that are being targeted.

However, whilst procedures like the above, and using anti-virus software and firewalls are very useful tactics, a more strategic approach is required. This involves conducting a risk assessment and developing and implementing a coherent security policy. Such a policy entails access control, crisis management planning (review chapter nine again), and compliance with legal standards. Access control should cover not only who accesses the system (and what parts they access), but other issues like the use of memory devices and attachments of various types. All of these actions need to be consolidated by comprehensive training and security policy updating.

One crucial aspect of e-commerce security is compliance with the UK Data Protection Act 1998. Although detailed advice should be obtained from the website of the Information Commissioner's Office, anyone who processes personal information must comply with the following 'eight principles'; that information is:

- Fairly and lawfully processed
- Processed for limited purposes
- Adequate, relevant and not excessive
- Accurate and up to date
- Not kept for longer than is necessary
- Processed in line with people's rights
- Held securely
- Not transferred to other countries without adequate protection

The essence of e-commerce

This section on e-commerce started with the statement by Meg Whitman that communications is at the heart of e-commerce. Communication consists of the creation, dissemination, interpretation and understanding of messages. Research has confirmed (e.g., the e-commerce Trust Study by Studio Archetype and Sapient & Cheskin) that the following messages are vital to the success of e-commerce:

Understanding   Showing the customer that needs and concerns have been identified and met (e.g., FAQs)

Presentation   Quality website design signals professionalism

Navigation   Easy access and clear instructions mean ease of use and effortless purchase

Explanation   How orders will be processed, and how problems will be addressed (e.g., policy statements)

Trust   Symbols such as Visa and Verisign, and testimonials convey security and trust

Brand image   This reinforces the messages of quality and trust, but also suggests good customer care

10.2 Internet marketing

The success of an e-commerce website does not just rely on product price, availability or range of goods or services. Like a traditional business, e-business success also depends upon developing consumer awareness through a strategic approach to marketing. Whilst traditional marketing has its place, the impact of traditional marketing suffers from the 'law of diminishing returns'. In other words, when specific marketing campaigns end, this often manifests itself in falling sales. However, the techniques of online marketing mean that the marketing message is continuous, constantly updated and efficiently targeted to meet particular consumer demands.

Internet marketing (also referred to as e-marketing or online marketing), is simply the marketing of goods and services over the internet. It includes all online techniques such as market research, product advertising, email marketing and direct sales. However, its impact is optimised when integrated with other means of communication like telephone technology, direct mail, promotions or face-to-face interaction. An indication of the overall value of internet marketing is the report by PricewaterhouseCooper that US advertisers spent some $16.9 billion dollars in 2006. Internet marketing can be seen to be associated with various types of businesses:

E-commerce   Goods are sold directly to consumers and businesses (B2C and B2B)

Advertising   Ads are sold to a variety of customers

Lead-based   Value is generated by selling sales leads from websites

Compared to traditional marketing, internet marketing can have a relatively low cost of entry. But it is not just low entry costs that make internet marketing so attractive, there are other cost advantages as well:

- Customers can be provided with much more information at minimum cost
- Many more customers can be reached at little, if any, additional cost

- Updating marketing material such as catalogues takes less time and less cost
- Targeting is made easier by having several electronic versions of the same material

Additional advantages include: reduced costs generally through automation and technology; more information means increased consumer choice, faster response times, better targeting; a vehicle for expanding from national to international markets; and a wealth of data to better meet customer needs and grow the business. Perhaps the biggest advantage of internet marketing is that consumers can research and purchase items at any time, anywhere in the world. All of these advantages mean that e-marketing is particularly suitable for small businesses.

Despite the above advantages, internet marketing also has a number of limitations: security issues, lack of face-to-face interaction, increased competition (the advantage of low cost of entry can also be a disadvantage) and complete dependence on technology. However, the dependency on technology should not be allowed to obscure the fact that, like traditional marketing, internet marketing must be based on an awareness of customer needs, buyer behaviour and maintaining customer loyalty.

In some respects, internet marketing makes maintaining the customer relationship a much easier proposition than is the case with traditional marketing. The relationship can be seen to consist of several elements: asking customers to register provides important information such as email addresses and business statistics; website facilities like email strengthens the relationship and provides important feedback; an FAQ (frequently asked questions) facility allows for better customer relationship management and is an important aspect of 'added value'.

Traffic-building (search engine optimisation) is an important feature of internet marketing, and consists of increasing the number of right visitors to a site so that marketing objectives can be achieved. Traffic-building is essentially about combining new online media channels with traditional offline communication techniques to optimise the online marketing message; there are two main aspects to traffic-building. Firstly, maximising the long-term strategy of bringing new visitors to the website (e.g., by using the web analytic tools mentioned earlier); secondly, using particular campaigns like product promotions to heighten interest. In both these strategies, information management is the key.

But where information is concerned, online marketers do not have things all their own way. Consumers can get information about product evaluations from neutral sites, chatboards and blogging sites (see section 10.4). The fact that much of this product comparison information is almost instantaneous and relatively cost-free means that online marketers have more pressures to get the key messages right (and in time), than traditional marketers.

Internet marketing can be viewed in terms of different types, such as *search engine marketing, email marketing, affiliate marketing, viral marketing* and *blog marketing*. The difference between these types is outlined below:

Search engine marketing (SEM)   A form of internet marketing that works by attempting to increase the visibility of business websites in the search engine results pages

Email marketing   A form of direct marketing that uses electronic mail as a means of communicating commercial messages

Affiliate marketing   A method of promoting web-based businesses in which the promoter or publisher (the affiliate) is rewarded for every lead/customer/subscriber or sale provided

Viral marketing   This term refers to a technique where social networks are used to heighten brand awareness. This form of marketing gets its name because it spreads in the same way as a virus

Blog marketing   Blog marketing takes the form of web logs where companies, using products and services as a basis, communicate interactively with customers

Search engine marketing (SEM) developed alongside the creation of search engines themselves. These were necessary to help people find information quickly, and to cope with the explosion of websites generally in the 1990s. So-called 'search engine optimisation consultants' emerged with the objective of helping businesses to utilise the marketing and advertising opportunities presented by search engines. The size of SEM alone in the US in 2006 is reported as $9.4 billion. Such figures suggest that SEM is growing faster than traditional advertising. The largest SEM vendors are Yahoo, Google, Search Marketing and Microsoft adCentre.

In a way, business emails are a form of marketing, since many will contain company logos or letterheads and be associated with a product or service. However, in a practical sense, the term email marketing is used to refer to: email that is sent with the specific purpose of enhancing the relationship between an e-tailer (a business that sells goods or services on the internet) and its customers; email that is sent with the specific purpose of generating sales; email that is sent with the express purpose of attracting new customers and retaining old ones. The American Direct Marketing Association estimated that US firms spent some $400 million on email marketing in 2006. Email marketing has the following advantages:

- Flexibility and low cost
- The email customer list is of great value in itself (e.g., a rich source of sales leads)
- It offers a direct contact with the customer
- Success rates can be efficiently tracked
- It is instant and can reach many potential customers
- It is an online form of traditional proactive marketing 'push' (websites have to 'pull' customers)

Despite the above advantages, the sheer volume of email, and email that is unsolicited (spam) have created a negative image for this form of internet marketing. One way around this problem is the development of 'opt-in' email. Here, the recipient has consented to receive the email. So-called 'permission marketing' works by the recipient ticking a box (or clicking etc.); a common example in this respect is an emailed newsletter highlighting company product events or promotions.

As well as affiliate marketing taking the form as described above, it is also the name of the business activity where different companies, affiliate networks or individuals conduct this particular form of internet marketing. These methods include free SEM, paid SEM and email marketing. Affiliate marketing, where one website is used to drive traffic to another, is often referred to as the 'stepchild' of online marketing.

The most active business sectors for affiliate marketing appear to be general retail, gambling and adult products and services. Although it is difficult to obtain precise figures for the revenue generated by affiliate marketing, it is estimated that in the UK, total sales for 2006 exceeded £2 billion. Revenue is generated in a number of ways such as cost per click and cost per sale. Merchants like affiliate marketing because they only tend to pay for results. Whilst some affiliate marketers have worked hard to improve their image over the last ten years, the industry is still criticised for lack of self-regulation and problems like spam.

Although the technique of viral marketing can be delivered by word of mouth, it is particularly powerful when the internet is used. Viral promotions are based on the willingness of people to pass on the marketing message voluntarily. The key here is to identify individuals or sites that have a high SNP (social networking potential), and create messages that are likely to appeal to these individuals or sites and be passed on. Viral campaigns can take the form of video clips, games, images and text. A recent example of viral marketing was the Cadbury's Gorilla advert being shown on YouTube and Facebook.

The value of Blogging in general has been recognised by both small businesses and major corporations, and this will be discussed in section 10.4. Where blogging as a marketing tool is concerned, the development by major players appears to be headed by Google through their Adsense programme. One of the main reasons why blogging is so potent is that it is the modern form of that most powerful marketing tool—word of mouth.

Though each has a part to play in the modern marketplace, the competition between traditional and online marketing is essentially a struggle between the old and the new. But it is not just about different techniques; there are also important conceptual differences between the two, and these are outlined in figure 65. Where online marketing is concerned, it is mostly the customer who initiates the process.

Consequently, the major challenge for online marketers is to maximise the limited time available by providing the maximum, relevant information.

Concept	Traditional Marketing	Online Marketing
Communication	One-way ('push')	Interactive ('pull')
Advertising space	Costly	Relatively inexpensive
Customer contact	Indirect	Direct
Brand image	Most important	Less important than information

Figure 65: The main differences between traditional & online marketing.

10.3 Using email effectively

Email is really the electronic version of the memo, and the evidence for this can be seen in the actual layout (e.g., 'To', 'From', 'Subject', 'CC'). Email has become an indispensable tool for business and personal communication on an international as well as national scale. In a business context, it is a significant tool for customer service management, registration and account information and finance-related information. In a personal context, it has simplified communication and increased its speed for millions of people worldwide; email has become a social medium as well as a technical tool. Email has other advantages:

- It is cheaper and quicker than a letter
- It is more interactive than written forms of communication

- It can take less time than a telephone call
- It allows the sender to highlight key points effectively
- It is easily retrievable and useful as a record

However, like other means of communication, email also has disadvantages: emotions cannot be conveyed (though emoticons are sometimes used to overcome this problem); there can be a mismatch in email systems between sender and receiver (what the sender sees on their screen, may not be the same image or format that the receiver sees); some employers are concerned that employee's interpersonal communication skills have suffered; like other computer-related aspects, security can become a key issue. Employee morale can also suffer, because the constant stream of emails mean that the sense of achievement is minimised. Despite these particular disadvantages, there is an additional one that causes serious concern to both companies and individuals—email overload.

An indication of the problem that email overload has become is that some estimates show that individuals can lose up to twentyone days a year just processing it; no wonder email is sometimes referred to as, *'the cholesterol of modern business'* In the business context, management consultants Mesmo estimate that organisations the size of European Commission can receive more than one million emails a day. But it is not just large businesses that suffer from email overload, some smaller enterprises have declared 'email bankruptcy', and have returned to traditional methods of communication. Some steps can be taken to minimise the problem of overload:

- Set the context of the email at the beginning (use the subject line)
- Use the pyramid writing structure (e.g., important information first, supporting detail, action required)
- Minimise the number of copies sent
- Minimise the use of 'reply to all'
- In general, use the KISS approach (keep it short & simple—make emails brief)
- Edit/summarise forwarded messages where possible
- Use templates for frequently used responses
- Use abbreviations, for example:
  FYI – for your information
  FYA – for your action
  RES – response required to a previous message
  QM – quick message
- Use hyperlinks (if colleagues are on a shared network, then attachments can be minimised; this also reduces file size). Further email abbreviations are outlined on page 166

In addition, it is best to check emails at set times rather than continually. Unless an important email is expected, switch off the 'new email' alert. Another important procedure to minimise overload is to adopt a priority strategy: delete the unimportant; create a 'pending folder' (emails that require a more considered approach); archive potentially important emails in date order.

Since managers also suffer from email overload, it is in their interests to take the lead in developing strategies to reduce the problem. Examples in this respect are: set and enforce maximum email file sizes, encourage the use of other channels of communication, establish a policy for email use, conduct email etiquette training.

Email and internet policies

An email policy is best enforced within a policy about use of the internet in general. An internet policy is now a prerequisite for any business, and good practice for any individual who uses its many benefits. A policy is necessary in order to protect the business from: damage to systems or information, legal action resulting from misuse or actions by employees or others, efficient use of resources and the reputation of the company. Any policy must be coherent and consist of the following elements:

- A clear and detailed outline of what practices are deemed to be acceptable and unacceptable
- A clear and detailed outline of what action will be taken if the policy is breached
- The communication of the above in writing when the employee starts their employment (the induction process) and reinforcement through company training programmes

A sensible approach for an organisation is to create a 'hierarchy of offences' that will be linked to their disciplinary process. For example, there is quite a difference between wasting company time on internet surfing or sending emails to friends, and downloading or distributing offensive or abusive material. However, as media reports have confirmed, even sending emails to friends or acquaintances (particularly of an intimate nature) can seriously affect the reputation of companies when these are copied and relayed throughout cyberspace. Serious breaches of company internet polices include:

- Downloading files that may contain viruses (by passing firewalls etc.)
- Breaching copyright
- Libelling or defaming others
- Downloading pornography or other offensive material
- Transmitting sensitive company data without authorisation or encryption

The increasing practice of employees working from home, or accessing company systems from home, can cause additional problems in terms of conforming to company internet policies. Companies can increase their protection here by instituting an Internet Acceptable Use Policy. Such a policy needs to set out: what is defined as personal use; what practices are not acceptable; again, what sanctions they may incur if policy is breached; that their computer usage at home may be monitored (e.g., what sites were visited, emails sent etc.). It is important that the company's internet policy is in writing and is signed by the employee on commencing employment (and updated after resuming employment where applicable).

It is vital that examples are given of material that is held as offensive, defamatory; and that breaches company regulations, or criminal or civil law. In addition, practical guidance needs to be given as to what constitutes personal use (and what amount if any, is allowed), how attachments are to be handled, and what steps are to be taken to prevent unauthorised use. A report by the CBI in June 2008 revealed that surfing the web by employees for personal use costs UK employers £10 billion a year.

Email etiquette (netiquette)

Businesses need to establish email etiquette procedures for three main reasons:

Professionalism   Every communication from an organisation sends explicit and implicit messages about how they conduct business, and related issues such as competence, standards and values.

Effectiveness   Maximum impact at minimal cost is one of the bywords of business. Emails that conform to the guidelines of: focus on the key issues, conciseness, accepted format, good grammar and spelling, and effective customer care help meet this byword. In doing so, emails also become a key vehicle for enhancing the business.

Risk management   Email is one of the most useful tools of the modern business, but at the same time, like general internet use, it can expose businesses to considerable risk. A properly designed, communicated and enforced EUP (email user policy) along with good netiquette can help reduce business risk.

As yet, there are no universal rules governing electronic communication, but some generally accepted good practices have emerged. This good practice is based on basic courtesy, respect for others, ethical behaviour and personal and company security. The following is a brief checklist of netiquette practice:

- Use the subject line effectively (it should summarise the message)
- Set the context if necessary, but keep it brief ('Reply to Sender' is useful, but do not over-do)
- Use the Cs of communication (e.g., clear, concise, courteous and comprehensible)
- Get grammar and spelling right, it sends messages about you and your company
- Do not use capitals for all text (in email terms, this is interpreted as 'shouting')
- Use spaces and breaks between paragraphs for clarity
- Keep acronyms, abbreviations and emoticons to a minimum
- Check attachments for viruses, and avoid long ones
- Keep signature files short (avoid graphics and favourite sayings)
- Use plain text and avoid colour etc.
- When emailing large groups, use the 'blind carbon copy' feature
- Avoid exposing any email lists you may have
- Use encryption software when sending sensitive business information
- Take care, people other than the recipient may see your email
- Check before you send as a matter of course!
- Never send an email when you are angry

Additional email 'shorthand'

2L8	too late
AAMOF	as a matter of fact
AFAIK	as far as I know
B4N	bye for now
CMIIW	correct me if I'm wrong
CUL	see you later
FWIW	for what it's worth

IKWUM	I know what you mean
IMHO	in my humble opinion
KWIM	know what I mean
ROTFL	rolling on the floor laughing
TIA	thanks in advance
TTYL	talk to you later
;)	happy
:(	sad
:	very surprised
;*	kiss

10.4 Blogging

Usually consisting of short, regularly updated postings, a blog is a web-based journal powered by a self-publishing tool; the word 'blog' is an abbreviation of the term, 'web log'. Blog postings are presented in reverse chronological order (the latest entry first), and each entry is dated and timed. The blog often contains links to other blogs or related online sources.

Blogging really took off in the late 1990s, when software was developed that made blogging much simpler to create and maintain than traditional web pages. A key feature that separates blog writing from other forms of online communication is their dynamic and interactive nature. Really successful blogs are those that have developed a unique 'voice' or writing style. In addition to the written type, blogs can take the form of podcasts, photographs or videos. The purpose of a blog is not always to generate the optimum number of 'hits', but to communicate with like-minded individuals.

Blogs work essentially by using an RSS (Really Simple Syndication) feed that can be read and viewed online (RSS uses a device called an *aggregator* to combine the feeds from all your favourite sites). Blogs have advantages over other internet techniques since they do not use email (thus, blogs do not lead to inbox clutter), and do not require formatting, special coding or templates. Yet another advantage of blogs is that information related to the chosen RSS feeds comes automatically. Although a newsreader is required, this is easily downloaded.

When an RSS news feed is updated, the newsreader produces a headline, short summary and a link back to the full text. An alternative to downloading blogging software to your computer is to sign up with a Web-based host such as Bloglines or Google Reader. In this process, you simply create an account and choose which feeds you are interested in; the website will create a

Mini Glossary

Podcast An audio file that is capable of being played by most computers and MP3 players. The RSS aggregator tool (or 'podcatcher') can automatically check for favourite podcasts and dowload them. The most popular aggregator is ITune (especially for music)

customised page for you that displays the relevant headlines. Despite the fact that web-based readers are not as fast as software-based systems, they have the advantage of being accessed from any internet-connected computer.

Decisions will have to be made as to whether you allow advertising from your blog web host in order to get a free account, and what blogging system to use. However, Yahoo Small Business offers a deal designed especially for bloggers, with the easy to use WordPress pre-installed.

Whilst statistics for blogging vary according to the source, US research conducted in 2004 showed that eight million adults had created blogs; blog readership stood at 58% (almost 30% of internet users); 12% of internet users posted comments on blogs. The phenomenal growth of blogging is evidenced by the fact that by the first quarter of 2005, nearly fifty million US internet users had accessed blog sites.

Blogs tend to fall into two main categories: *personal blogs* (a mixture of a personal diary approach, opinions and research interests with associated links), and *business blogs* (an organisational tool for communicating with customers and employees). Compared to traditional media that need a long lead-in time, blogs are a form of instant publishing.

Business blogs should not be seen as a rival to e-newsletters, but as a complementary business communication device. Whereas the e-newsletter is a valuable business tool, the blog has more immediacy, is more interactive and comments can be added to it. Because blogging requires no experience of web html or expensive consultants, business blogging is a low cost alternative to having a web presence, and this is particularly important for small companies.

In addition, business blogs offer a more informal and approachable way to gain and give information about the company, its culture, products and service issues. In short, a business blog provides a voice for the business that informs and educates existing and potential customers and employees. Cleverly composed, blogs can also be an important competitive advantage.

Further advantages of business blogging include:

- Project co-ordination (e.g., keeping people informed about the status and progress of projects)
- Crisis management
- Addressing FAQs (frequently asked questions)
- Facilitating changes and data updating
- Providing a 'human face' for the company (e.g., a video blog by the owner or chief executive)
- Building trust
- Achieving faster recognition by search engines

Blogs can be a mixture of information, opinions, business-related comment and links to related issues; unlike web pages, they can be easily updated. Since blogs are short, chatty and interactive, they are more likely to elicit a response than traditional marketing communication. Consequently, they are, potentially, a powerful tool for marketing and promotion. Research in 2005, by Hostway, an American web-hosting and internet services company, found that 45% of respondents held that blogs were more credible than TV commercials; 45% felt that blogs were more believable than internet advertising; and 41% viewed blogs as more convincing than radio advertising.

However, most internet experts agree that the case for the use of blogging as a prime direct-response marketing tool still has to be proven. What is not in doubt, is the business blog's ability to build crucial customer relationships, increase brand awareness, improve networking capability and intensify the business dialogue

Despite the above advantages, there are also dangers for companies who use blogs: disaffected employees can criticise the business, and customers can complain about products and bad service.

Nevertheless, negative comments can also help identify key issues regarding employee morale and motivation, identify training needs, generate in-company ideas and innovations, and focus the company on key business issues.

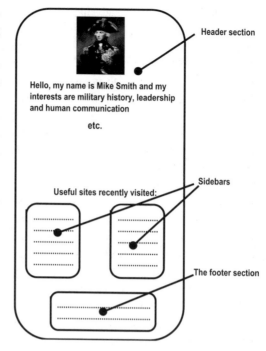

Figure 66: Key elements of a blog.

Key elements of a blog

The header   Likened to the masthead of a newspaper, the header is the first thing a person sees when they enter your weblog. Whether it takes the form of text or graphics (or both, as in figure 66), it needs to be catchy and, at the same time, represent what your weblog is about. Blog headers often contain links to other items such as an RSS feed or other pages of your site

Sidebars   As figure 66 again illustrates, most blogs follow a two or three column format, with the main column taking up most of the space. Sidebars can contain a mixture of things such as FAQs, a favourite quote, links to other sites or a search box

Posts   The blog post or entry is the main feature of the blog, and should be strongly emphasised. Great care needs to be taken regarding the font used for the posts (it must be easily readable), and in addition, the posts must be easy to navigate. Posts can contain a number of things, and the following are examples:
- the post title (the headline for your entry)
- the date and time
- links and credits (links to other sources should always be acknowledged)
- the 'pull quote' (an interesting phrase from a source you have linked to)
- your blog name (this should be linked to an email address)
- A permalink (this links the post to a web address in your archives)
- the 'add comments' link (this allows visitors to post comments about your entries

The footer Many bloggers add a footer to their page; this can contain a number of items, from the comments system used, to a web counter

The business blogger's checklist ✓

- Be clear what the purpose of your blog is
- Identify your potential audience and customer base
- Make your site easy to navigate (e.g., use targeted words in your entry titles)
- Develop key messages (especially your USPs—unique selling points)
- Communicate information in an interesting way
- Register with blog search engines
- Register with tracking services
- Consider trading some links (this could boost your site traffic)
- Use the KISS approach where entries are concerned
- Try to develop a personal blog writing style (this may take time)
- Use clear, relevant titles for each posting
- Keep your blog up-to-date
- Offer incentives to encourage business traffic (e.g., small prizes, free products)
- Engage in 'blogrolling' (links on your blog site to internet sites of related interest)
- Network—comment on other blogger's comments
- Monitor your traffic (e.g., are there consistent themes; do you need to vary content or style?)

Summary

- The immense sums associated with internet business transactions (e.g., the purchase of Skype by ebay) highlight the incredible value of e-commerce and the crucial role that communication plays in this context
- In the world of e-commerce, a well designed website is essential for success. Research has confirmed that potential customers view the following as very important:
  - detailed information about the product
  - detailed information about the seller
  - price comparisons
  - information about the security of the transaction
- In order to optimise the potential of e-commerce, customer databases are invaluable
- Like a traditional business, e-commerce success also depends upon a strategic approach to marketing. Internet marketing has advantages such as:
  - many more customers can be reached at minimum cost
  - customer targeting is easier
  - more information can be provided
  - updating material is easier and cheaper
- In a business context, email is a significant tool for customer service management, account handling, and greatly speeding up the communication process. Establishing and reinforcing email policies is critical for performance
- A blog is a web-based journal powered by a self-publishing tool. The purpose of a blog is not always to generate the optimum number of hits, but to communicate with like-minded individuals

- Key advantages of blogging are its dynamic and interactive nature, it does not use email, and no special knowledge is required of coding or formatting techniques. Further advantages of blogging include:
  - project co-ordination
  - crisis management
  - a 'human face' for the company
  - building trust
  - addressing FAQs
  - facilitating change (e.g., responding to customers comments)

Tutorial

1. a. If you or your company already have a business website, evaluate its effectiveness using the criteria on pages 135 & 136 (e.g., how easy is it to navigate? what information is provided? how reassured will the potential customer be regarding the security of transactions?)

   b. If you do not have a business website, then using a DIY package, create one using the above criteria

2. a. Using the information provided below, develop a profile of 10 key customers in a chosen organisation:
   - purchase history
   - service history
   - account history
   - age, income and lifestyle

   b. Develop and refine a marketing promotion that would appeal to the customers selected

3. Using the information provided by a sample customer base you have access to, and using the 'eight principles' of the Data Protection Act 1998, assess how the principles have been adhered to

4. Apply the principles of email etiquette to your emails; how do you rate on a score from 1–10?

5. Using the information provided on pages 145 & 146, design a business blog

Index